JOHN DEERE
NEW GENERATION
TRACTORS

Chester Peterson Jr. & Rod Beemer

MBI Publishing Company

We proudly dedicate this book—
which details one of the greatest innovations in agricultural machinery history—
to all the truly great and talented people at Deere & Company, past, present, and, yes, future.

Acknowledgments

These people contributed greatly to this work and richly deserve—and have—our sincere thanks: William (Bill) Hewitt, retired president and CEO, Deere & Company; Les Stegh, archivist, Deere & Company; Michael Mack, retired director of the product engineering center, Deere & Company; Harold Brock, retired director of the product engineering center, Deere & Company; Harlan Van Gerpen, Warren Wiele, Danny Gleeson, and Jack Decker, retired engineers, Deere & Company; Fred Hileman, retired Deere & Company employee; and Jack Cherry, editor, *Two-Cylinder* magazine.

We also express our appreciation to that great fraternity, the restorers and collectors of John Deere New Generation tractors, those enlightened ones who have ventured beyond the venerated two-cylinder John Deere—and who often went out of their way to help with photography and providing us with information. Members of this group are Randy Addington, Larry Angtal, Ernie Burbrink, Kevin Burbrink, Dwight Emstrom, Wayne Findley, Leah Goecker, Randy Griffin, Michael Gross, Nathan Hill, Mike Hoffman, Walter and Bruce Keller, Jon Kinzenbaw, Paul and Nick Kleiber, Glen Knudson, Mel Kopf, Ken Lang, Larry Maasdam, Jeff McManus, Dennis Polk, Jack Purinton, Darold Sindt, Kenny Smith, Duane Starr, Ron Stauffer, Brian Thompson, and Doyle Whitney.

And a special thanks to one of the leading catalysts of the "Ageless Iron" movement, *Successful Farming's* Dave Movitz.

First published in 1998 by MBI Publishing Company, 729 Prospect Avenue, PO Box 1, Osceola, WI 54020-0001 USA

© Chester Peterson Jr. & Rod Beemer, 1998

The information in this book is true and complete to the best of our knowledge. All recommendations are made without any guarantee on the part of the author or Publisher, who also disclaim any liability incurred in connection with the use of this data or specific details.

MBI Publishing Company books are also available at discounts in bulk quantity for industrial or sales-promotional use. For details write to Special Sales Manager at Motorbooks International Wholesalers & Distributors, 729 Prospect Avenue, Osceola, WI 54020-0001 USA.

Library of Congress Cataloging-in-Publication Data

Peterson, Chester, Jr.
    John Deere new generation tractors/Chester Peterson, Jr. & Rod Beemer.
        p. cm.—(Farm tractor color history)
    Includes index.
    ISBN 0-7603-0427-0 (pbk. : alk. paper)
    1. John Deere tractors. I. Beemer, Rod. II. Title.
III.Series: farm tractor color history.
TL233.6.J64P48   1998
629.225'2—dc21   98-25570

On the front cover: The 4010 was a huge step forward and one of the most popular tractors in the New Generation series. It won the hearts of farmers the world over with its exceptional balance of horsepower, fine operating manners, and tasteful styling.

On the frontispiece: This particular 4620 Diesel model had many unique features and options, such as front-wheel assist, three SCVs (Selective Control Valves), lighting packages, quick hitches, and factory-installed cabs. John Deere engineers developed turbocharging and intercooling technology on this model, systems which forced more cooled air and fuel into the combustion chamber producing substantially more horsepower.

On the title page: The 1010s offered several options including power steering, independent dual-speed 540 rpm and 1,000 rpm PTOs, dual rear rockshaft, and one remote cylinder hydraulic system. In addition, there were many different front ends available for the various 1010s, including an offset seat and chassis arrangement that gave the driver a clear view down to the soil.

On the back cover: Top: The 4000 Low Profile Diesel majestically poses behind its siblings at a show. It uses a fixed tread front axle from a 3020 Row-Crop Utility tractor factory-installed in the short-wheelbase position. ***Bottom:*** The 3010 and 4010 New Generation tractors were the first of their model designation to roll off the factory production line. The 3010 was available in row-crop, standard, row-crop utility, special row-crop utility, and grove and orchard tractor versions, while the 4010 was offered in standard, special standard, row-crop, row-crop utility, hi-crop, and industrial versions.

Edited by Paul Johnson

Printed in Hong Kong through World Print, Ltd.

Contents

INTRODUCTION

It's difficult to think of the John Deere New Generation tractors as already old and seasoned enough to become highly sought-after collectibles. That's because such a high percentage of them are still out there doing their thing, plowing, planting, and harvesting—and still looking as modern as any tractor on four wheels. But when we do the math, it surprises us to realize they've been around for four decades.

For some of us, the sight and sound of a John Deere D, a Case SC, a Ford-Ferguson 9N, or an International Harvester M bring back fond memories. Those were the tractors many of us spent endless hours operating and that we learned to love, and occasionally hate.

Now a new generation of farmers and others express those same feelings for the tractors of the 1960s, a decade kicked off by the John Deere New Generation tractors.

What exactly constitutes a New Generation tractor is open to friendly debate. Some people, for example Bill Hewitt, consider only the initial tractors introduced as the "New Generation" of tractors. Others, including the authors, feel that all the new models and later refinements of the introductory tractors through 1972 can truly be defined as John Deere New Generation tractors.

Incidentally, by the middle to late 1960s, the Deere & Company worldwide tractor program was in place. Models coming out of its foreign facilities had similar specifications and looks to the tractors manufactured in the United States.

When John Deere introduced its New Generation of tractors in Dallas, Texas, August 30, 1960, it crisply defined Deere & Company's basic philosophy. In the process, the company also redefined the standards for all other agricultural tractor manufacturers.

It's a great story. It has challenge, intrigue, personalities, humor, and certainly, success. Here you're going to find information about these pace-setting tractors. Undoubtedly, as interest in the New Generation tractors continues to escalate, additional chapters will need to be written as more information unfolds.

PREFACE
The Old Generation

Certainly in the 131 years between the establishment of John Deere's first blacksmith shop in Leicester, Vermont, to the introduction of the "New Generation" tractors in Dallas, Texas, there were numerous events that could be termed as defining moments for the company.

However, introduction of its New Generation line can arguably be called "the" defining event. It was a bold, even radical, departure from Deere & Company's policy that had served it so well for more than a century.

The company's history reveals a pattern that trailed behind founder John Deere, who began as a blacksmith, like an unbroken thread throughout his life. Move . . . associate with another man or firm . . . move again . . . associate with another man or firm . . . buy a firm . . . then move . . . .

Deere left New England for Grand Detour, Illinois in 1837. One of his first jobs there was to mend the broken pitman shaft on a sawmill owned by Leonard Andrus. Only a few short months later, Deere reached one of the critical defining moments in his life: fabricating his first plow utilizing a steel saw blade. His plows scoured well in the wet, sticky soil of the Midwestern prairie and were quite successful.

Deere and Andrus soon entered into an informal business arrangement. In 1843, they modified this into a formal partnership, agreeing that the business would operate under the name, "L. Andrus."

This partnership dissolved five years later in 1848 when Deere foresaw a need for better transportation, especially since the railroad was bypassing Grand Detour. Following his established *modus operandi*, Deere embarked on another series of partnerships, and yet another series of financial trials.

Deere's choice for the location of his next business was Moline, Illinois. In addition to railroad facilities, the town was also located at the confluence of the Mississippi and Rock Rivers.

Making use of Moline's extensive transportation facilities proved to be a sound business decision. This final of Deere's many physical plant moves lasted not only for the rest of his lifetime, but has endured for the succeeding century and a half.

However, the move didn't result in the last of Deere's partnerships. He immediately signed an agreement with Robert N. Tate. The name over the door now read Deere & Tate. This was soon out of date as John Gould joined the budding partnership. Production of plows began in 1848 and grew rapidly.

Tate and Gould eventually departed. Finally, the firm was reorganized in 1868 and incorporated as Deere & Company with Deere and his son, Charles, as equal owners. Deere at this point was 64 years old. His entrepreneurial efforts had run through numerous different partnerships over 47 years to at last culminate in the corporation that now so proudly bears his name.

The succeeding decades could rightly be called the "foundational" years of the growing Deere & Company. It now was incorporated, had a strong record of production, and had enough history to give it direction. Charles Deere was in charge as the CEO.

During the ensuing years under his guidance, several policies were implemented that early on established Deere & Company as a leader in farm implement production and sales.

Although contrary to popular belief, John Deere didn't invent the first steel plow. However, what he did with the steel plow concept in terms of quality and improvements was significant. This established a precedent that the company has followed throughout its history.

Also significant in shaping the company's philosophy has been staying ever mindful of the needs of farmers. This is illustrated by Deere & Company's move toward an expanded line of equipment in 1851.

Another business ingredient that Deere & Company recognized early on was the need for ease of distribution. In other words, management asked, how useful is a product if the company can't get it to the consumer without undue complication and expenditure of both time and money?

In those bygone days, the local merchant or "dealer" who handled a manufacturer's product had little tie or loyalty to the company. And, usually the merchant had the option of selling just one item or a full line. Even more surprising, a merchant could sell a competing manufacturer's equipment, guided in this decision only by his interests or whims.

Breaking new ground, in 1869 Charles Deere opened the first Deere & Company branch house. It was followed by four more during the next two decades. The branch house concept tied the marketing organization to the parent company either as a wholly-owned subsidiary or through other financial or management arrangements.

By making this move, Deere & Company continued the tradition of emphasis on strong sales that John Deere had followed from the outset of his career.

The upshot: Deere & Company could now provide a full line of equipment plus full-service dealerships for the benefit of farmers. This may have been one of the most significant moves of many that Charles Deere contributed to the company—and to the entire industry.

Over the years, Deere & Company evaluated and kept close tabs on the needs and wants of the potential buyers of its products. The company realized it paid to keep a finger on the pulse of the buyers.

Then, if Deere & Company wasn't producing something farmers wanted, it actively sought out manufacturers who were making the desired piece of equipment. The next step was to decide which manufacturer was producing the best such product. Finally, Deere & Company would make the move to either buy outright, buy controlling interest, or by some other arrangement, bring the desired product into its equipment line.

Yet another principle that's guided the company through the decades has been its patience. Offsetting John Deere's personal drive and impatience to get the job done in the blacksmith shop or factory, has been his namesake company's extreme corporate patience in product development.

By the turn of the century, farm power was rapidly changing thanks to the new internal combustion engine. Company after company furiously rushed tractors to market. Even then, however, Deere & Company followed its usual cautious, conservative approach to new products: wait, evaluate, and let others spend time and money on research and development.

Soon though, the company's own branch house dealers were pressuring for a tractor to add to the Deere & Company array of equipment.

Both Case and International Harvester were heavily promoting tractor research and development. This caused farmers to begin to look to these manufacturers for their farm implements, too.

In 1912, the Deere & Company board of directors decided to develop a tractor plow. C. H. Melvin was given the job of producing the first experimental model. One tractor was built, a three-plow, three-wheeler. For whatever reason, though, work on this tractor stopped in 1914.

That same year, Joseph Dain Sr. was instructed to produce a tractor that could be sold to farmers for approximately $700. The

---

FIVE GENERATIONS OF DEERE & COMPANY MANAGEMENT
1837–1982

Some member of the Deere family headed the company for its first 145 years, a most singular accomplishment:

John Deere: (1804–1886) Founder 1837; Director 1868–1886; President 1869–1886.

Charles H. Deere: (1837–1907) Director 1868–1907; President 1886–1907; Second son, fourth child of John Deere.

William Butterworth: (1864–1936) President 1908–1927; Married Katherine Deere, daughter of Charles Deere.

Charles Deere Wiman: (1892–1955) President 1928–1942, 1944–1955; Grandson of Charles Deere, son of Anna Deere and William D. Wiman (While Charles Wiman served in the U.S. Army 1942–1944, Burton F. Peek filled the company presidency during his absence.).

William (Bill) Hewitt: (1914–1998) President and CEO 1955–1964; Chairman and CEO 1964–1982; Son-in-law of Charles Deere Wiman through his marriage to Patricia Deere Wiman.

Dain All-Wheel-Drive tractor was the first production tractor to bear the now famous John Deere name.

Again, though, Deere & Company followed the conservative path of careful testing, pricing, and studying the competition. Orders were issued in 1917 to build just 100 of the Dain tractors.

However, in early 1918 Deere & Company bought the Waterloo Gasoline Tractor Company. This decision was again consistent with past company expansion efforts: research the best available and add it to the Deere & Company line through some sort of acquisition.

The Waterloo was modified through several model changes until the famous Model D was adopted for production in 1922. For 20 years, the "Johnny Popper" or "Johnny Put-Put" gained market share. It was always second to International Harvester in sales, but it continued to both sell and work well.

During this post-World War II boom period, hardly anybody envisioned the two-cylinder Deere becoming obsolete—that is hardly anybody except the management at Deere & Company. In the late 1940s and early 1950s, farms continued to get larger, which in turn resulted in a need for ever more powerful tractors.

Deere & Company's competition was happily providing farmers with four- and six-cylinder engine tractors. Meanwhile, the engineers at Deere & Company continued bringing out larger two-cylinder models that were continually redesigned to incorporate state of the art refinements.

But, there was growing and justifiable concern at Deere & Company that the two-cylinder engine design was approaching its limits and a size too large to be practical. The market was demanding a power-to-weight ratio that could be achieved only with a change to a four- or six-cylinder engine.

It was time for Deere & Company to break with tradition. In 1953, the decision was made to replace the faithful two-cylinder tractors with an across-the-board line of new tractors.

Notwithstanding the impressive growth and success of the past, Deere & Company had reached one of its most—if not the most—definitive moments in company history.

This 1962 4010 Diesel Row-Crop has a narrow front end so that with a mounted cornpicker, it could go down between the rows without knocking down any corn. This tractor was built only with Synchro Range transmission. A 4010 could have either a narrow front end or a wide front end and still be considered a Row-Crop tractor. Both the rear and front wheels can be adjusted for width on the Row-Crop.

Breaking Tradition

John Deere gave his company an important guiding principle that appeared frequently in early company literature. Charles Deere included this principle in the Deere & Company 1860 catalog:

"The determination of the proprietors to improve rather than deteriorate on their already acknowledged superiority of manufacturing will be a sufficient guarantee to all that every exertion will be made to furnish promptly a superior article at a low figure."

Eighty years later, one word in the above credo assumed unprecedented importance for Deere & Company. It was *deteriorate*. Viewed against the new, more powerful multicylinder tractor lines of its competitors, the two-cylinder–powered tractor faced serious deterioration in its ability to meet the needs of future tractors in a rapidly changing agricultural scene.

Deere's entrance into production of the two-cylinder tractor was based on factors that were justifiable and appropriate to the market in 1918. During that time, George Peek gave the Deere & Company board of directors reasons why a two-cylinder was acceptable, even superior, to a four-cylinder engine. His report itemized these six reasons:

1st. A two-cylinder tractor can be built cheaper than a four and price is an important factor, because the tractor is a business machine and must win by its economy.

2nd. The tractor, unlike the automobile, must pull hard all the time. The bearing must be adjusted for wear. There are half as many bearings to adjust on a two-cylinder tractor and half as many valves to grind.

3rd. There are less parts to get out of order and cause delay.

4th. The bearings are more accessible on a two-cylinder horizontal engine than a four-cylinder vertical engine.

5th. Two-cylinder engines will burn kerosene better than fours.

6th. Four-cylinders are not necessary on tractors. The fact that a tractor is geared 50 to 1 instead of 4 to 1 eliminates all jerky motion. The engine of a tractor can be made heavy and have a heavy flywheel and can be mounted on a strong rigid frame. Therefore, a two-cylinder engine is satisfactory in a tractor and when it is, why go to the four-cylinder type.

During the early 1930s, International Harvester and Allis Chalmers were able to offer both a wheel-type tractor and a crawler (track-laying) tractor. The competition had a distinct marketing advantage over Deere & Company tractors in certain farming areas with large acreage under tillage, as well as in varying soil conditions and terrain.

West Coast farmers preferred, even demanded, track-laying tractors on their huge

Both these New Generation tractors carry the lowest serial number assigned by John Deere to New Generation tractors: No. 1000. This means they were the first 3010 and 4010—the foundation of the New Generation line—to start down the Waterloo, Iowa, factory assembly line and go out the door in 1960.

farms that more often than not contained areas of semimarshy soil. Crawlers were a distinct advantage in the hilly terrain of the large orchards in the Pacific Northwest.

Perhaps the first test of the commitment to the two-cylinder engine came as a result of Deere & Company's joint marketing effort with Caterpillar.

At this point neither Deere & Company nor Caterpillar could offer its dealers, especially in California, a complete tractor line to their customers. Deere & Company didn't produce a track-laying model, and Caterpillar had no wheel tractor.

In 1935, the two companies agreed to conduct a joint marketing effort. Certain concerns were justified by people on both sides. Deere & Company had to be a confident company; loyalty wasn't ignored when it was a matter of selling either a crawler or a wheel tractor.

The preeminent concern was voiced from Caterpillar's headquarters, however, in a bulletin to its sales organizations. This bulletin, in part, read:

> The builders of John Deere tractors have been particularly consistent in regard to the design of their engines. . . . [T]wo-cylinder design is now exclusively a John Deere feature. In selling the John Deere tractor, Caterpillar salesmen may be met with the sales argument that all other tractor manufacturers building two-cylinder tractors have discontinued this feature.

Caterpillar wasn't suggesting that the two-cylinder was obsolete. In fact, the company had one-, two-, three-, four-, six-, and eight-cylinder engines in its line, which had a worldwide reputation for excellent quality.

The bulletin presented an interesting spin on the salability of the two-cylinder

This attractive matched trio of "20 Series" New Generation models includes a 1969 2520, a 1969 3020, and a 1964 4020. The 1964 4020 with Power Shift was the first built, and so it is rather unique.

engine as an asset for both Deere & Company and Caterpillar:

> Inasmuch as the "Caterpillar" salesman has been trained to sell exclusive features . . . he should welcome these exclusive John Deere features as sales opportunities.

The logic was certainly sound. John Deere was exclusively building and selling two-cylinder tractors for 42 years. They are affectionately called "Johnny Poppers," due to their distinct exhaust note. A few years later, though, Deere & Company was forced into a defensive posture by its competition.

Year after year, the competition circulated rumors that Deere & Company was discontinuing the two-cylinder, all in an effort to convince potential customers that the two-cylinder was obsolete.

In 1937, L. A. Rowland, vice president and general manager, apparently felt compelled to respond with this field service bulletin—and, yes, the upper case words are his:

> A Four-Cylinder Engine—Not On Your Life
>
> Some of our dealer and tractor owner friends occasionally tell us they have heard that John Deere is coming out with a four-cylinder engine in all John Deere tractors. Dealers and others who are well-informed know that this rumor is false.
>
> We want to assure those who are not so well-informed that we are NOT coming out with a four-cylinder engine. THE JOHN DEERE TWO-CYLINDER ENGINE HAS BEEN SO OUTSTANDINGLY SUCCESSFUL THAT THERE IS NO THOUGHT OF A CHANGE.

Wow! He couldn't have been more specific or emphatic in denial, could he? Yet the thought of change wasn't too long in presenting itself to company thinkers.

During the decade following Rowland's bulletin, the tractor replaced approximately 20 million horses as draft power for farming per year. Labor unions increased wages in the urban industrial centers, drawing farm labor away from the farms to factory jobs.

GIs returning from World War II, many of them from small rural farming communities adopted a "bigger is better" philosophy that helped the Allies defeat the Axis powers of Germany and Japan.

They were used to bigger aircraft, bigger armies, bigger tanks—doing everything on a grand scale.

After World War II, it was a global "seller's market" for most goods and services. The expanding export market for American products, including farm commodities, fueled a rapid expansion in innovative research and manufacturing.

There's some indication that by the late 1940s, company engineers were thinking of replacing the two-cylinder with a four-cylinder model. By 1950, they actually produced a mock-up of a four-cylinder unit based on the Waterloo A frame.

This tractor never proceeded further

This is an impressive all-star line-up of New Generation models. From left, a 3020 diesel, a 4010 diesel, a 4000 gas, a 4020 diesel, a 4320 diesel, a 5020 modified with a 275-horsepower Detroit Diesel V-8, and a 5050 that was a 5020 until converted to a 400 horsepower Cummins diesel.

than the mock-up stage, however. To gain insight and information, some engineers installed a General Motors (GM) diesel in a Case LA tractor and then field tested it in the Great Plains wheat belt.

Once again, Deere & Company went to farmers to find out just how much bigger and better the farm tractor of the future should be.

Deere's modus operandi of asking questions of the end user, the farmer, provided company management with vital information on which to conduct their decision-making process.

Remember, at this time—1949 to 1950—the average tractor (from all tractor manufacturers) provided a rather modest 29 horsepower.

Research conducted with the one-of-a-kind Case-GM hybrid tractor led to the conclusion that wheat farmers both could and would use greater tractor power in their farming operations if it was available. Actually, what they wanted was more power than any agriculture tractor commercially available at the time.

Assimilating this information, the marketing people visualized an opportunity for Deere & Company to provide a completely new tractor. This tractor would furnish more power, plus feature the latest technology in engines, transmissions, and operator comforts.

Such a new tractor would complement Deere & Company's equipment line that was gaining increasing market share against industry leader International Harvester.

So it really wasn't a question of whether or not the company needed a new, more powerful tractor. Management was in agreement that it was essential. Instead, the debate focused on the merits of power from an upgraded two-cylinder versus a radical departure into the unfamiliar territory of the three-, four-, or six-cylinder tractors.

Through continued upgrading of its two-cylinder tractor line, Deere maintained a respectable market share and a remarkably sound customer loyalty. The

The "cut-away" 4010 even has an exposed area in the Row-Crop narrow front end. Difficult to see on the outside, there were inside improvements here, too, compared to the previous Row-Crop models.

Model A introduced in 1934 brought two firsts to the industry: adjustable wheel tread and a one-piece transmission case. It also came with a power lift that converted it from a mechanical to a hydraulic system.

The workhorse of the Deere fleet was introduced in 1923—the Model D. Throughout its life, many improvements were made to it, including rubber tires, electric starter, and lights. In 1940, the Model D was given a horsepower increase to meet the demands of large acreage farmers in the wheat belt.

The Model R, a landmark tractor in its own right, was introduced in 1949 and was the first Deere & Company tractor to be powered by a diesel engine. It generated just 34 drawbar horsepower, however.

International Harvester introduced the first successful diesel agricultural tractor in 1933, which was 16 years before the initial Deere & Company offering. IH stood in stark contrast to Deere, holding a position far ahead of Deere in that area.

Concerns began to arise as to how large the two-cylinder could become as it increased in horsepower before exceeding the practical physical size limits of such an engine. For this reason alone, development of a four- or six-cylinder vertical engine with higher rpm capacity seemed inevitable. But the two-cylinder still had an ardent corps of advocates at Deere & Company headquarters and down on the farm.

It was time for Deere & Company to play catch-up. Clearly, a more aggressive tractor program had to be adopted.

Charles Deere Wiman was a great-grandson of John Deere by marriage and was a member of the board from 1919 to 1955. He served as vice president from 1924 to 1928, after which he assumed the presidency. During World War II, from 1942 to 1944, he served as a colonel in the U.S. Army. He resumed his previous position as president in 1944 and worked until his death in 1955.

It was during Wiman's tenure that debate surrounding the two-cylinder models intensified; however, during the war and Wiman's absence, the "cylinder-count" issue was relegated to a relatively low priority.

The nation going to war put responsibilities on all manufacturing facilities to do their part for the duration. Deere & Company responded with production of various war material. The emphasis was to switch from machinery output to military production.

This led to another subject that pestered all manufacturers: war quotas. Another impact was a shift from decentralization—a Deere & Company hallmark—to a more centralized operation better able to deal with war production.

Immediately following Wiman's return to Deere & Company, he launched an aggressive expansion program with a small, low-cost tractor at the top of the list. Still the "cylinder-count" question remained, although it wasn't a top goal.

In January 1945, the company purchased land in Dubuque, Iowa, for the construction of a tractor plant with which to build its Model M. The plant began producing the tractor in 1947.

In the same year, Deere & Company also purchased the Des Moines ordnance plant, meanwhile expanding its plants in Moline, Illinois, and Waterloo and Ottumwa, Iowa. This flurry of activity and rapid expansion was in response to the pent-up demand for farm machinery expressed during the immediate postwar years.

Alleged, or feared, obsolescence of its current stable of tractors was kept at bay during these years by ongoing engineering advancements on existing models. Yet by the late 1940s, it became obvious that Deere would surely jeopardize both future status and sales of its tractor lines, and possibly equipment lines too, unless a firm commitment was reached on the engine issue.

As the decade of the 1950s opened, the company faced three choices:
- Continue with minor engineering advances, coupled with cosmetic design changes, on the existing tractor line.
- Plan for major changes around the two-cylinder concept.
- Move decisively to scrap the existing models and make a commitment to models with more than two cylinders.

This was to be a decision with huge implications for the entire organization. After all, the tractor works was the leading profit-maker. A long shutdown for the factory to change over to an entirely new line of tractors was a risky proposition.

By this time, Wiman was in favor of phasing out the two-cylinder as long as profits were high on the two-cylinder. It demanded considerable vision and faith to embrace a total change. He also realized it would take years to bring the new tractor on line, and in the meantime, tractor innovations and production must be kept current of demand if sales were to remain strong.

Nothing is forever; however, improvements were designed, engineered, and incorporated as if the two-cylinder surely would continue forever. Sales were good and the customers satisfied.

But the "Deere dilemma" of two-cylinder versus multicylinder engines debate wouldn't go away. By 1953, it was apparent to most of those in management positions that the two-cylinder had reached its maximum potential, although it had to service Deere customers for another seven years.

Nobody in the company, except the employees working directly on what was to become known as the New Generation project, knew that they were seeing a small sampling of the New Generation technology on the middle and late 1950s two-cylinders. These features appeared in some of the 20 and 30 Series tractors.

Of course these items of necessity were just "samplings." The firm of Henry Dreyfuss made real innovations in human factor-designing. Operator comfort and control was a high priority. Accordingly, the firm of Henry Dreyfuss had been kept secret until the new tractor was ready to be introduced.

Security surrounding the development of what was to become the New Generation line of tractors dictated that many records had to be destroyed so they wouldn't fall into the competition's hands. Unfortunately, this secrecy practice meant that much of the historical detail is gone forever.

In 1953, it's well established that a firm decision was made to replace the two-cylinder with a line of four- and six-cylinder tractors. In that same year, President and CEO Charles Wiman was diagnosed with a terminal illness and died in 1955.

His son-in-law, retired President and CEO Bill Hewitt, recalls that during the two years of Wiman's terminal illness the necessary research and experimentation demanded by the "more cylinder" project languished.

According to Hewitt, it was Wiman's decision to proceed with the development of the four- and six-cylinder tractors. It was

Open viewing of the tractor's rear end on the right side was available also. It was possible to see the mechanism work as the tractor was rolled or towed forward.

made without input from the board of directors, which was a break from traditional Deere & Company policy.

Hewitt concurred with his father-in-law and stated that the two-cylinder mainstay should be replaced with engines with more cylinders.

In 1953, Wiman authorized an ambitious research and development program to make the new tractor a reality. It was a monumental decision, and certainly a defining moment in Deere & Company history. It was a gutsy move and a departure from the highly profitable, more comfortable "number two" market position in the tractor industry. Wiman put the entire company on the line.

There was no company to research and buy in this case, so there was no product innovation to borrow from others. In addition, there wasn't a current model to use as a base for continual improvement.

Management personnel, marketing people, product engineers, and production experts faced the job of peering years into the future. They had to anticipate what the new tractor should provide to farmers to

match the demands of the rapidly changing world of agribusiness.

Wiman had broken with company history and tradition. Deere & Company was about to enter into new territory.

Bill Hewitt was Deere & Company President and CEO during the New Generation tractor's conception, gestation, and birth. Fortunately, he was already convinced that the risk involved in designing and producing new four- and six-cylinder tractors was substantial—but that the risk of sticking with only two-cylinder tractors was much greater. The time had come to make the change.

"I was an executive who was interested in getting in on the leading edge of competition. I got interested in everything that would make Deere & Company a stronger competitor.

"When I first went to work as CEO, Deere & Company had, proportionately, the best earnings in the industry. To be sure, at that time International Harvester was a lot bigger. But proportionately Deere & Company was more profitable.

"The old-timers also had sort of an

Six cylinders, count 'em, triple the number of the ol' Johnny Put-Put. John Deere wanted everybody—from those inside the company to farmers—to understand that the New Generation tractors were different and an advancement. A special "cut-away" 4010 was furnished to each sales branch for demonstration and education purposes. This 4010 was made for the Omaha, Nebraska, branch, and later was used in the Kansas City, Missouri, branch when the two branches merged.

unwritten rule that Deere & Company was happy being a strong number two to International Harvester. Let International Harvester be the "ice-breaker . . ."

"My attitude was quite different. I'd been in the U.S. Navy for four years during World War II. I observed, after the war was over, that the pace of change had accelerated considerably. What do I mean by that? A

lot of things," said Hewitt.

"All of these changes were also accelerating much faster. I'd tell them in management meetings, 'Look, we can't afford the luxury of being a strong number two to International Harvester any longer. The pace has changed and the pace is so much more rapid. Now by the time International Harvester does something that's recognized, it's

too late for us to catch up with them.

" 'So, if we want to be leaders in this industry, we've got to spot the trends, decide which trends are good, and then get in on the leading edge of the trend.' "

Deere & Company was ahead of all other manufacturers in returns on dollar investment from its tractor line. The old philosophy notwithstanding, the company had maintained an active research and development program. This effort resulted in constant improvements on the existing models in its line.

When then President and CEO Wiman initiated the changeover order in 1953, the tractor line could boast some excellent models. The line saw major advancements the previous year. This was when the first numbered models replaced the lettered models.

John Deere's Two-Cylinder Line-Up

To set the scene for the later New Generation tractors, consider that the two-cylinder Model 50 that made 20 drawbar horsepower and 26 belt horsepower replaced the Model B, which originally was rated at 9 drawbar horsepower and 14 belt horsepower. Through constant improvements to the gasoline B, it eventually tested out at 19 drawbar horsepower and 24 belt horsepower in 1947.

Introduced in 1934, the Model A was originally rated at 16.22 drawbar horsepower and 23.52 belt horsepower. But the 1947 tests of the gas model delivered 26.48 drawbar horsepower and 33.53 belt horsepower. It was replaced by the Model 60 at 27.71 drawbar horsepower and 35.33 belt horsepower.

The Model 70 Diesel came aboard in 1953 with 34.25 drawbar horsepower and 43.77 belt horsepower. It was comparable to the Model R Diesel, which was rated at 34.27 drawbar horsepower and 43.32 belt horsepower in Nebraska tests in 1949.

Additional tractors came on-line in 1953 to take the place of the previous letter models. The Model 40S Standard, 40T Tricycle, and 40C Crawler replaced the M, MT, and MC. The 40 Series produced a modest jump in horsepower over its predecessors.

For example, the 40 Tricycle was listed as 17.16 drawbar horsepower and 21.45 belt horsepower. This compares favorably to the M at 14.39 drawbar and 18.21 belt horsepower. The 40 Standard tested at 16.77 drawbar horsepower and 21.13 belt horsepower, while the MT was rated at

When new, this "cutaway" could be powered up with a special electric motor that enabled most of the engine parts to move as they did in a regular engine. It was both an effective demonstration and teaching device concerning the New Generation's design and power.

14.08 drawbar horsepower and 18.33 belt horsepower.

Comparing the crawlers, the 40C was at 15.11 drawbar horsepower and 21.24 belt horsepower. This was slightly more than the MC at 13.70 drawbar horsepower and 18.89 belt horsepower.

The horsepower tests alone demonstrated little advantage of the first numbered tractors over their predecessors; however, horsepower tests alone didn't reveal the entire story. The new numbered models had benefited from Dreyfuss' design input. This created a much greater comfort factor for the operator, plus much-improved overall styling.

The 50 Model introduced duplex carburetion—a separate carburetor for each cylinder—to improve both fuel efficiency and horsepower. The new model series of numbered tractors were the first John Deere units to have live powershafts to provide continuous power for Power Take Off (PTO)-driven equipment.

The first row-crop John Deere diesel

was the Model 70, also released in 1953. It set a new fuel economy record.

This series also improved the hydraulics with the high-pressure Powr-Trol system that could handle heavier drawn or integral loads and operate independently of the PTO and transmission clutch. These tractors were the first to offer LP models and the Hi-Crop models too.

They also had improved steering, better seats, and improved operator refinements such as longer clutch and throttle levers. Rack-and-pinion rear wheel tread adjustment made changing the rear wheel tread a quick and easy job. At the time these tractors were introduced in the early 1950s, they were equal to any tractor in the industry.

After the new two-cylinder line had been introduced with industry leading advancements, it demanded great determination and foresight for the company leaders, and especially the engineering team, to look ahead. They had to envision a tractor that would eclipse all the models of all manufac-

If one two-cylinder tractor doesn't have the power, why not rig up a way to harness two of the two-cylinder tractors together? The coming of the John Deere New Generation tractors with their modern powerplants made such on-farm modifications unnecessary.

turers—and do it seven years into the future!

It was evident that it was going to be difficult to keep personnel working on current tractor advancements while others were diverted to the effort of developing the new, multicylinder line. Deere & Company couldn't risk falling behind on the models that were to go head-to-head with the competition until the new tractors were ready years in the future.

Management and engineering met the challenge with the 20 Series in 1956 and then followed with the 30 Series in 1958. Horsepower increases and advancements in almost every aspect of design and engineering kept Deere & Company a solid number two to its longtime competitor, International Harvester.

Then, in 1959, Deere & Company introduced what could later be thought

were placed within somewhat constraining and restrictive parameters. They had to increase the available horsepower, yet not to the level of the 8010 tractor. They were also tasked with improving the concept and styling of the company's new tractors, but not so radically that farmers would hesitate to buy them.

Then, to raise the bar even higher, Hewitt said Deere & Company would no longer accept the number two position among agricultural equipment manufacturers. Deere & Company's goal was to assume the mantle of number one.

Hewitt has some recollections concerning his perspective about the New Generation tractor project: "Wiman got the project initiated and on the move, while I was the new 'getter-doner' CEO. My thought was, 'Well, okay, the ball is now rolling. So, let's shift from first gear, to second gear, and to third gear and then to high gear and get the thing designed and field-tested and produced.' "

New conceptual ideas are almost always linked to, and initially limited by, what has gone before. When discovering the new, it's usually necessary to rethink and reexamine the old. The New Generation tractor concept was no different.

While nobody knew what would eventually take shape on the blank sheet of paper, it was recognized by management that whatever was developed absolutely must be kept secret.

This was necessary to protect sales of Deere & Company's current line of tractors. If potential customers knew the tractor they were considering buying was going to be obsolete in one, two, or three years, they'd most likely put off buying it, or worse yet, they might go to the competition.

Two things quickly became apparent. First, personnel couldn't carry on the new development work simultaneously with their current duties required on existing models. Second, if secrecy was to be maintained, the project needed to be moved to a remote location. That way only those people involved with the project would have access to the ongoing developments.

of as the harbinger of the New Generation tractors yet to come—the awesome 8010. This tractor was a quantum leap ahead of the competition. In fact, many of its features are just now finding their way onto production models of all makes.

Today, huge articulated four-wheel-drive tractors with 200-plus horsepower are the norm. But at the time, the 8010

seemed to be too much for the average farmer to either grasp or buy.

Farmers would flock to demonstrations to see this unique-looking monster turning over soil with so many plows and yet with such effortless ease. A shortage of customers for the new 8010 forced Deere to rent or lease most of the small number of 8010s that went out the door.

Designers of the New Generation tractor

These two-cylinder John Deere tractors are in storage south of the Waterloo, Iowa, Deere & Company plant. They were stockpiled to fulfill customer needs while the plant was shut down for approximately six months to change tooling and the assembly lines over to manufacturing the New Generation tractors.

vided spectacular performance. So, experimentally, V-4, V-6, and V-8 engines were married to the Model A frame; however, these engines proved too wide. The engine cowlings were so wide that operator vision was reduced to unacceptable levels.

To determine the operator's field of vision, a small spotlight was mounted on the tractor in the same location that the operator's eyes would be. Then in a darkened room the light was turned on, and an engineer marked the shadow line in chalk on the floor. It wasn't exactly high tech, but the method was effective. The V-engine idea was eventually rejected.

Some work was also done using a horizontal four-cylinder powerplant. It, too, proved unacceptable. Many new transmission concepts were developed and tested—and scrapped.

Was this effort all trial and error without focus? No, the blank sheet of paper approach allowed plenty of room for the trying of new concepts. Regardless, the program was still focused at achieving concrete results within certain parameters.

For instance, the design of the new tractor would have to be able to accommodate existing two-cylinder tractor

An empty supermarket was leased in downtown Waterloo, Iowa, in 1953. It became the engineering center for initial work on the New Generation tractors. Veterans of the project still refer to the facility as the "meat market."

The worldwide Deere & Company PEC (Product Engineering Center) was occupied in 1956 under the direction of Merlin Hansen. Many at Deere & Company consider him to be the real father of the New Generation tractors.

Design was managed by Wally Dushane and development by Don Wielage. Key designers included Sid Olsen, engines; Vern Rugen, transmissions; Danny Gleeson, chassis and controls; Ed Fletcher, hydraulics; and Chris Hess, hitch.

The first shop building had been completed two years earlier, in 1954, and at that time the project started being moved

out of the former grocery store to these new facilities.

Early prototypes used existing frames, wheels, and other items from the current two-cylinder tractor family.

During this period, the V-8 engine was extremely popular in automobiles and pro-

This is a "V" engine mock-up of a New Generation tractor. The photograph was taken some time between 1950—when Deere & Company was designing an in-line four-cylinder engine on a Model A frame—and 1954 when experimentation was conducted with four- and six-cylinder "V" engines.

William (Bill) A. Hewitt (1914–1998) was Deere & Company president and CEO under whose leadership the New Generation of tractors was developed and introduced. He served as director from 1951 to 1982, executive vice president from 1954 to 1955, president from 1955 to 1964, and chairman and CEO from 1964 to 1982.

Charles D. Wiman (1892–1955) director, 1919–1955; assistant secretary, 1922–1924; vice president, 1924–1928; president, 1928–1942 and 1944–1955. In 1953, Wiman made the decision that Deere & Company would develop a completely new line of multicylinder tractors.

implements. Farm implements were becoming so big and heavy, and it was deemed desirable to design a system that would be easier for one man to attach and detach the implements.

Increased horsepower and greater efficiency for the small farm acreage, as well as the vast tracts such as wheatland operations, was vital.

Operator comfort and convenience was a major design priority as well. Advanced hydraulics to power and manage the increased demands of equipment had to be addressed along with PTO-powered implements.

Industrial designer Dreyfuss had had limited involvement with Deere & Company tractor styling since 1935, but the New Generation's blank sheet of paper concept allowed him the first real opportunity to influence the total overall design of a tractor.

Influencing much more than just the shape of the tractor itself, he also brought new thinking to what came to be called the increasingly important human factor: operator comfort and ease of tractor operation.

To accomplish all that the criteria dictated required coordination and cooperation from the entire Deere & Company organization. Everything started with Hewitt, of course.

He frequented the PEC facility and field demonstrations to watch, evaluate, and offer input. His feedback was considered, not just because he was CEO, but because as CEO he was the man who kept the project focused. And, intuitively, he was often right.

Engineering and manufacturing worked together to ensure that everything that was designed could be manufactured with efficiency and cost effectiveness.

Marketing and sales were kept in the loop, because they knew the most about the competition they'd be selling the new tractors against. They also had a feel for what customers would lay out their hard-earned cash to purchase. And it worked, with no surprises. Well, all right, maybe a few surprises.

Seven years can be a long time or a very short time. If you're waiting to win the lottery, seven years is a long time. If you're designing a new tractor line, seven years can be an extremely short time.

Signaling the end of its era, this Model 430 was the last tractor manufactured by Deere & Company that used the reliable, but increasingly out-of-date and underpowered, two-cylinder engine.

Each part of the new tractor needs to be designed, engineered, and built as a prototype. Then it must be thoroughly checked out in the test cells where dynamometers can verify horsepower and durability. Transmissions, hydraulic systems, frame and structure, electrical systems, and PTOs all had to make it from concept to drawing board to prototype before finally becoming integrated as a complete tractor. Provided it passes these harsh tests, the new tractor must then be field tested in the same actual conditions that the product will later operate under in real life.

Finally, once a design has been accepted and proved, manufacturing must decide how it will be produced. Only then can orders for buying and installing the necessary tooling or manufacturing machinery be ac-

quired or built to produce the new tractor.

It's important to keep the time factor in mind to fully appreciate the New Generation tractor's development.

The engineers who were part of the team that produced it have some surprising insights and interesting war stories.

For instance, their immediate response to the question, What was the most significant design advancement on the entire New Generation line? is, "The hydraulic system has to be right up there near or at the top."

What this new system permitted was having more power-assisted functions supplied by one central pump. Deere & Company wasn't merely trying to catch up to the competition in this case. The new pump, according to the engineers that designed it, allowed the New Generation tractor to pull

way ahead of the competition.

At this time, conventional gear pumps were only capable of maintaining 1,000 psi. Deere's new eight-piston pump design could deliver 20 gallons a minute at 2,000 psi.

The rock shaft and power steering cylinders could be smaller while still providing adequate power for the job. It was a definite benefit. In addition, the new pump was economical to produce. It was also more forgiving than other pump designs when contaminates entered the oil.

The closed-center system offered power on demand to the tractor's power steering, power brakes, and three-point hitch, as well as remote cylinders. And, also important, when the system wasn't in use, it required minimal power drain from the engine, only approximately 1.5 horsepower.

The transmission and differential case was the reservoir for the system. This design was made possible by specially designed oil, which served as the hydraulic fluid and gear lubricant. Equipped with a system filter and oil cooler, the new hydraulics were well-suited to be touted later as a "New Generation of Power."

Hewitt also pointed out that in the early 1950s, the average horsepower of farm tractors was in the area of 35 horsepower. Today, it may require 35 horsepower just to operate the hydraulic system while under load.

Michael Mack, former director of the Product Engineering Center, pointed to a cylinder block on the line at today's Deere & Company Waterloo Engine Works and indicated that the cylinders were "sacred ground." He explained that when the engines were first designed for the New Generation tractors, someone had to determine the center line dimensions of the block, which would locate the cylinders.

Once this was determined and fixed, the tooling that would fix the boring spindles on those centers was ordered. If the engine design didn't work, the boring patterns for the cylinders would be changed. This meant the corresponding tooling would have to be changed too.

There are many reasons the word *sacred* is used when referring to cylinder dimensions. Not considering the time required to reorder tooling and install it, the price of changing such an engine line in today's dollars would carry a price tag around $70 million.

For the record, Deere & Company is still using those same fixed-cylinder center dimensions on its tractor engines manufactured today. This is a great tribute to the New Generation engineers.

Some of the original New Generation tractors—3010 and 4010—also introduced a new transmission. Not only was this transmission new in tractor design, it was designed in a revolutionary way that impacted the entire gear manufacturing industry. Harlan W. Van Gerpen was an engineer at Deere & Company who worked on gear design for the new tractor. Back in the

1950s, gear design was laid out on a drawing board and the corresponding math was worked out on a calculator.

Van Gerpen and Mack explain that even for an engineer well versed in this design and math, it would take six to eight hours just to do the calculations on one set of gears. They also had to calculate all numbers to the eighth decimal place.

To put it in layman's terms, the critical design of gears is matching the gearset so both gears have the same strength. The teeth of the two gears are different in design, with one having a wide base or root, the other being slightly undercut at the root. It's at this point failure will occur if one gear is weaker than the other.

Van Gerpen realized that computers might be able to do this burdensome job quicker and more effectively than humans. His problem was that no computers were yet available to the engineers. Deere & Company had just installed a 650 IBM at their headquarters in Moline, Illinois, though.

Remember that this was in the era of punch cards, plus Moline was three hours away by automobile. The new machine was in constant use during the day. Van Gerpen didn't view this as an insurmountable obstacle, however. Armed with his belief, he'd drive to Moline after work in Waterloo, then spend the night there working on his program to design gears by computer.

The payoff came when he finally was able to bring his completed design and math back to Waterloo. There, his work was compared for accuracy with designs and computation worked out by the old method: success.

Not only was the math correct to the eighth decimal place, but the computer could accomplish it all in just 15 minutes, instead of the hours doing the work by hand demanded.

So Van Gerpen won the honor of writing the very first computer program for computer gear design. Later, of course, such computerization would become standard for the agricultural, automobile, and other industries all over the world. Development

of the New Generation tractor sparked the process.

Another benefit of this program was that the computer could design a gearset that could deliver 20 percent more power through the gears without risk of gear failure.

Yes, quite a legacy resulted from the New Generation.

Van Gerpen today heads a worldwide engineering and consulting firm that specializes in gear and spline design, gearing software, and test equipment. He notes that the design for the same gears that took six to eight hours to run by hand took only 15 minutes to process on the old IBM back then. Today, it can be accomplished in 5 seconds or less.

Field testing the landmark tractor revealed what worked and what didn't. Some of the testing provided some laughs along the way. Early design and production models had the PTO control lever located on the left side of the tractor near the console. The lever curved slightly outward at the top to allow the operator's hand to clear the console when engaging or disengaging the PTO.

After examining the controls and operator's platform, a company executive dismounted the tractor on the left side. In the process the back of his suit coat became hooked over the PTO lever. When he stepped to the ground, his coat became vented all the way up to the collar.

Intuitively, the attending engineers knew that a "suggestion" would soon be made to move the PTO lever to the right side of the tractor. It was, and they did.

Tractor and equipment testing was certainly not new to Deere & Company engineers. This "stepped it up a notch" with the New Generation tractors.

The PEC featured the latest in test equipment, from dynamometers to laboratories, from cold rooms to test tracks, and from tilting platforms to farmland. The experimental tractors were subjected to it all. Would the New Generation tractor hold up to the task of rigorous farm work?

Engines were hooked to dynamometers in the test cells and run day and night

An engineer sits at a drafting table creating the blue prints for the ergonomically correct New Generation tractor. By conducting extensive research and development, New Generation tractors provided an unprecedented level of comfort, allowing farmers to operate the tractor for hours without becoming fatigued.

Engineers conducted early styling and design, which determined the overall look of the New Generation tractor. From the finished mock-ups, molds and dies were made for fabrication of sheet metal parts.

for thousands of hours to measure both power output and durability. Afterward, the engines were disassembled and examined part by part for signs of excessive wear or malfunction.

The cold room could drop the temperature to minus 30 degrees Fahrenheit. This enabled the engineers to test the starting systems and other functions in extreme cold conditions.

The tilting platform is just that: a platform on which the tractor is mounted and then tilted. This is used to determine the stability of the tractor and how the various systems such as the cooling system, hydraulics, and engine lubricating system function at extreme inclined angles.

Loads are mounted on the three-point system and cycled up and down relentlessly hour after hour, day after day to ensure dependability for the buying customer.

Outside the test cells, tractors are hooked to wheeled dynamometers that are towed around test tracks in all types of weather, day and night, simulating various loads to measure power and performance. An outdoor mud bath checked the effectiveness of seals on wheels and axle bearings as the unit was driven back and forth, hour after hour.

Then it's on to the obstacle course where tractor and implements are relentlessly bounced over obstacles far rougher than would be experienced in most farming operations.

The Waterloo PEC boasts a state-of-the-art testing facility; however, Mack remains convinced that no matter how much testing is done at the facility, there is no viable substitute for field testing under real farming conditions.

To provide this final examination, Deere & Company field-tested the New Generation at its test farm near the Waterloo facility. The tractors were also hauled to several locations around the country including Texas, Arkansas, and Utah.

By the time the New Generation tractor was introduced in Dallas, its thorough testing equaled the equivalent of 10 years of average wear and tear, according to the engineers.

Rigorous testing is part of the R&D program. A tractor is subjected to continuous operation over many hours while in the mud bath to check the seal and bearing durability.

Keeping the secret during all this activity required some rather, well, call them *innovative* measures. Naturally, the tractors were always covered or enclosed during transport to test facilities. Test models were sometimes, if not always, painted red instead of green. In addition, there's some evidence that side panels were bolted to the tractors to hide the distinctive New Generation profile.

The entire process was later billed as the best kept industrial secret ever; however, there were clues around if people were paying attention.

Retired Deere & Company engineer Warren Wiele mentioned one such clue. When engines were placed in the PEC test pods, or cells, for dynamometer testing, the exhaust was vented through the roof of the building.

Deere & Company's two-cylinder engines produce the distinct exhaust noise that led to the nickname "Johnny Popper." In fact, on a calm day a John Deere two-cylinder working under load can be clearly heard a mile away. The exhaust notes of the four- and six-cylinder engines are distinctly different.

Apparently though, nobody ever picked up on this obvious clue and investigated what was producing the unusual sound.

The experimental tractors were constructed from a combination of parts fabricated by Deere & Company and parts outsourced from other firms. Purchasing personnel were careful to use many different suppliers to eliminate the possibility that any

Engines were placed in test cells, hooked to dynamometers, and run day and night for thousands of hours to measure both power output and durability. Test engines were regularly disassembled and analyzed for potential problems. According to engineers, this testing equaled the equivalent of 10 years of average operation.

This tractor was a sort of "new generation" tractor in its time. That's because it was the first tractor carrying the John Deere name to be powered by a two-cylinder engine. Deere & Company's previous two-cylinder tractor was marketed under the Waterloo Boy name.

one supplier could recognize a whole new tractor design. On at least one occasion, however, these special parts created some suspicion.

A camshaft for one of the six-cylinder engines was ordered from an out-of-state firm. The owner of the firm happened to have a brother who owned the local John Deere dealership.

Visiting his brother's firm, the John Deere dealer innocently inquired, "How's business?" and "What's that?" The state of the business isn't recorded, but the item in question was a camshaft destined for Deere & Company. The dealer was savvy enough to recognize that this camshaft was

definitely not for the traditional two-cylinder engine.

When he asked his brother what Deere & Company was going to do with a cam like that, his brother could honestly say he didn't know. The dealer didn't press the issue. It's likely that after D-Day in Dallas he remembered the incident and realized that he was one of the first people to see a camshaft made for the New Generation tractors.

Once the New Generation was successfully launched, another major event got underway in the Deere & Company engineering department. The worldwide concept that was to influence the succeeding models of New Generation tractors began at the

PEC in 1962. Harold Brock was chief engineer at that time.

"So, our next program was to design a 'worldwide' tractor at Waterloo," he explained. "Dubuque made one kind of tractor. Mannheim, Germany, was making tractors of another design. And both of these differed from the concept of the 3010 and 4010. So we said, 'We need a worldwide tractor, one that will satisfy the world.'

"Deere & Company had in the past been accused by many other countries of designing a tractor primarily for the Blackhawk County, Iowa, area. To combat this, we brought the engineers from these different Deere factories into

The tilting table is the tool that John Deere engineers use to test the roll-over threshold of prototype tractors. These tests define the safety limits for John Deere tractors that will be in the public's hands.

Waterloo, and we sat down and planned what would satisfy their market as well as the U.S.A. market.

"Our purpose was to determine what kind of a product would be best for markets on a worldwide basis. That's when the 1020 and 2020 series were developed. This was a rather unique experience, because it kind of set the standard for the world.

"In Germany, if you machined a part from our U.S.A. prints, it would turn out to be the opposite hand of it, or reversed. So we realized we needed drawings that wouldn't have to be converted by any factory.

"Incidentally, under the current system, when they converted our inch/decimal system into millimeters/metric, they had to round off the numbers. Sometimes then

precision parts wouldn't always fit, because they couldn't be rounded off evenly.

"We set out to make drawings that wouldn't have to be redrawn, and from which any Deere & Company factory in the world could make the part. This was the foundation of our worldwide concept of drawings. Germany and the other countries agreed to use our projection for the drawing format.

"We simplified it further by using symbols—another Dreyfuss contribution—on the drawings instead of notes in German, French, Spanish, or Italian. So if a part had to be round or square or linear, you wouldn't be reading this, instead you'd see a symbol.

"Then we decided to design in even millimeters, but also to put in the odd decimal equivalent. So, this way whatever ma-

chines they were working with, either inch or metric, they could be machined from the print without converting.

"In addition, all materials specified on the drawings were in even metric numbers, ensuring that all gauges were the same throughout the world. So that was the start of a worldwide design of tractors."

Four decades later, the emotion is still discernible in Michael Mack's voice as he tells about an engineering problem encountered with the 1020 and 2020 tractor models. It was only four short months before these models were to go into production, and the tooling specs had already been released.

Hewitt and the marketing team recognized that the gear noise was excessive. In fact, after further testing and observation, it was agreed that the noise was at a level that would make marketing difficult, if not impossible.

The tractor model had already endured months of testing and proved itself to be extremely durable. The problem was the load-induced noise. All facets of the tractor were acceptable under no-load operation. But, as soon as it was placed under a load, the noise level increased until it was unacceptable to the operator.

Mack said they tried everything available in a gear engineer's black bag of tricks. Nothing alleviated the noise. And there was no time left to redesign the entire gearbox. The engineers worked day and night attempting to resolve the problem.

Certainly Mack and his engineers probably viewed the situation from the aspect of their careers as being on the line. They were also concerned about the big picture: the new line plus all that was riding for Deere & Company on this new tractor.

The solution wasn't found on the drawing board or in adding decimal places. Finally, not because of mathematical formula or textbook learning but strictly on intuition, Mack and his engineers changed the gears from straight-cut to helical. Same diameter gear, same number of teeth, but helical.

The new helical gears were finally reassembled and installed into the tractor around midnight one night, and the tractor was immediately moved to the test plot behind the PEC.

They grabbed flashlights and proceeded to the field. Mack, flashlight in hand, followed the tractor into the night and gave the signal to engage the plow. Emotion filled his voice as he recalls, "Whisper quiet, it was absolutely whisper quiet!"

The nagging problem was solved. Except, there was no time left for the extensive testing that was required when specifications were altered. Again Mack and his en-

gineers made an intuitive decision: go with the new helical gear design. In retrospect, it was the right decision. A smidgen of intuition became an indispensable ingredient in the New Generation story.

Did the New Generation tractor design and engineering set a new benchmark for agricultural tractors? Most assuredly. Was it flawless? No. Few first-year vehicles built from the ground up are flawless.

Problems plagued the service people immediately after customers began buying and using the tractors. Deere & Company's reputation for outstanding service was put to the test.

Fred Hileman, service manager at the John Deere Waterloo Works, was instructed to do everything possible to get field service problems fixed immediately. The company didn't want anything to adversely affect early sales of the New Generation line of tractors. At the first indication of a field problem, the branch houses would be notified so they could immediately alert the dealers concerning the problem.

Some hydraulic fluid leakage situations cropped up, and there were approximately 150 tractors on which the differential carrier failed.

The most bothersome problem concerned water pump leakage. This persisted for at least two years after initial introduction. The situation became serious enough to warrant the Deere & Company board of directors to issue an invitation for engineering and service personnel to appear before the board.

During his presentation to the board, Hileman mentioned how Ford was dealing with a problem that required replacing the entire tractor except the tires and wheels.

He was no doubt referring to the problems Ford had with its tractor's new transmission. A simple, rather than an extensive, remedy was sought. He used the analogy of an aspirin: A cost-effective fix would be more desirable than major surgery, which would be a serious financial setback for the company.

The cylinder block was the culprit, which was causing the water pumps to leak. Sand from the casting process remained in the block during the entire machining process. After some hours of engine operation, the sand would eventually contaminate the cooling system. Once it began circulating through the system, it eroded the seals of the water pump.

A small ceramic insert was designed and installed as a field service solution until the casting process could be corrected.

This situation produced some friction among the different Deere & Company departments. An example of these strained relationships is commented on in a company publication, *John Deere Company: Kansas City Branch*, published in conjunction with its 125th anniversary:

> For example, at a branch house dealer meeting when problems were serious, the Waterloo Tractor Company's Service Manager, during a speech, advised the dealers that the problems were all their fault, because dealer service personnel were not clean enough with their shop work. At the time, the big problem was repeated water pump failure.
>
> One quite sharp dealer spoke up quickly after dealer service shops were accused of causing the problems. He asked, "Why did every water pump on every new tractor that we sold fail? Those tractors had not been in our shop except for pre-delivery servicing and, of course, during that time, the water pumps were never touched."
>
> The dealer who posed this question did have a point since he had sold 39 of the New Generation 3010 and 4010 tractors at that time.

Because of Deere & Company's commitment to its customers, the problems were eventually corrected through effort and cooperation from top to bottom within the company.

New Generation Horsepower Output

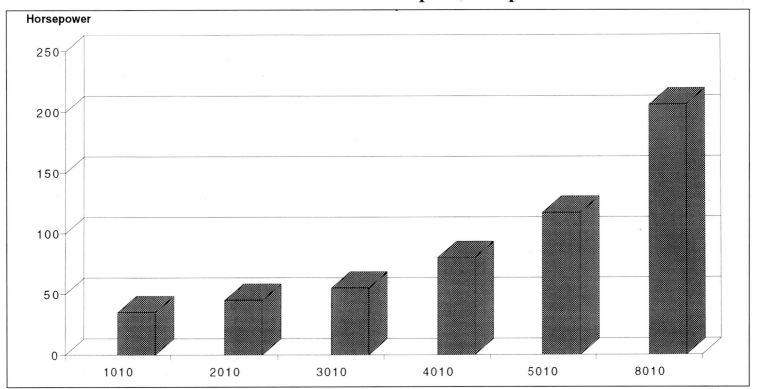

The horsepower of each of the New Generation tractors stair steps for the first three models, and then jumps a bit faster for the next three models. Spec sheets report that horsepower ranged from 35 in the 1010 to 206 in the 8010.

"10' series tractors	
Tractor	**P.T.O. H.P.**
1010	35
2010	45
3010	55
4010	80
5010	117
8010	206

2

STYLE & COMFORT

As a pioneer in industrial design, Henry Dreyfuss helped change the "shape" of our world.

For 44 years he designed and styled hundreds of products found in homes, including the Princess and Trimline telephones, Hoover vacuum cleaners, the familiar round Honeywell thermostat, cameras, sewing machines, washing machines, and a host of other everyday products.

He also designed locomotives for the New York Central railroad. The "Strategy Room" for the Joint Chiefs of Staff of the United States Armed Forces was also his design. And, he had been contributing to Deere & Company tractor design.

During these years, however, he'd been limited to making minor improvements to existing models without the opportunity to instigate a complete redesign.

With the New Generation tractor he was able to focus all his talents, thanks to the blank sheet of paper concept. In effect, he had impact on the tractor from the beginning. His input wasn't limited to just styling the shape of the hood or the curve of the fenders. The idea of improved operator comfort and operator control fell under the heading of what was later to be called the "human factor."

Hewitt recalled that Dreyfuss and members of his staff frequently visited the Waterloo and Dubuque plants. They had a complete understanding of the tractor's purpose. The word "design" in this instance included the mechanical performance of the machine as well as styling and operator safety.

According to Hewitt, "Henry Dreyfuss was concerned about combining styling, operator comfort, and operator convenience. Convenience in this case means that you can see the gauges and the dials without bending around the steering wheel to peer at them. They all must be visible by the tractor operator."

Dreyfuss paid attention to these details. He had worked for Deere & Company since 1935, and he understood that for most farmers a tractor was a major investment. He also noted that the farmer's wife would usually accompany her husband to the dealership when he was thinking of purchasing a new tractor. She wanted to see where he was going to spend all this money.

"Henry came to an interesting conclusion," Hewitt said. "Let's assume that two competitive tractor companies each have the horsepower and capacity that you want. Both of them are theoretically equal in mechanical performance, serviceability, in short, similar in every facet. But one of the tractors is a lot better looking than the other. They're both in the same price range. So, which tractor are you going to buy—especially if your wife's along with you?" Hewitt knew Dreyfuss was right about that observation.

At first glance, these model 3010 and 4010 tractors look real. (And, most restorers wish that they could locate similar New Generation tractors that were just as inexpensive.) It's sometimes easier to note and appreciate styling differences in life-like models than in the real thing. Note how designers made these tractors so much different and vastly more appealing—to both farmers and their wives who often accompanied them to the dealers—than previous models.

Note the cleanness of design and how "modern" it appears in contrast to the two-cylinder tractors that preceded it out Deere & Company's tractor factories.

Another change that Dreyfuss instigated was in tractor seat design. Hewitt said the common tractor seats of that era were known as "saddle seats." Hewitt's description is "a piece of extremely heavy sheet metal that was pressed, more or less in the form to accommodate your butt. There was no cushion at all. The seat had perforations for ventilation that read, 'Deere & Company.' And, in those days I used to say, 'Our name really makes an impression on the operators!' Finally, the engineers developed movable pads that they put on the seats."

Dreyfuss was responsible for gaining the insights of human posture specialist Dr. Janet Travell. Dreyfuss hired her to go out to the fields and watch the engineers operate their equipment. "She put on coveralls,

got on the tractors, and worked with them," Hewitt said. "Of course, some of the old die-hards commented that, 'This is no place for a woman.'"

Hewitt recalled one story that is probably still talked about within the company. One particular old-timer was lamenting the fact that Travell was out in the field working alongside the men. He said, "I remember the days when we designed tractor seats by having Ol' Sam sit in some plaster of Paris. He had the biggest butt in the factory, and his form became the shape of the tractor seat!"

Hewitt said Travell brought intelligent design to tractor seat design. "She knew just where the armrests should be, the dimensions of the armrests, and the amount of

softness or firmness in the armrests. She also set where the backrest should be in two levels—down at the bottom and another one up in the middle of the back area. And the flat seat now had foam rubber underneath the covering. This new seat was both firmer underneath for pelvic bones and softer underneath for thighs near the knees. She also had the engineers design a spring-loaded seat, so that the seat was not rigidly attached to the hard part of the tractor."

Because Dreyfuss had also observed the differences in farmers' sizes and weights, the engineers designed an adjustable spring tension for the seat that was lever operated.

Deere engineers were very serious about making the best possible seat. To test the seat's suspension, engineers at the Moline facility mounted the experimental suspension on a vibrating platform. Electrical test equipment was attached to the seat to measure the amount of vibration and shock that was transmitted from the platform to the seat. By analyzing the data from these tests, engineers were able to improve the suspension design to give a more comfortable ride.

These tests also revealed that the maximum safe up-and-down movement of the seat was 4 inches. Movement greater than 4 inches jeopardized the ability of the operator to remain on the seat and to control the operation of the tractor.

As America moved into the "push-button" age of postwar prosperity, Deere correctly anticipated that farmers would soon be demanding more comfort and convenience in the products they purchased. Cast-iron seats and knuckle-busting controls were quickly losing favor with farmers.

In the home, the hard, rigid, straight-backed chair was giving way to the upholstered recliner. So company engineers reasoned that the tractor operator who spends far more time on his or her tractor seat than sitting in a living room chair would appreciate operator comfort and convenience. Not only that, but the tractor operator is also willing to pay for enhanced comfort.

The deluxe seat was initially offered as a $50 option. Soon 95 percent of Deere & Company's customers were paying for this extra comfort, and the deluxe seat became standard equipment.

Marketing people grind their teeth at the mention of a "cab," because to them this is considered an "enclosure" or a "body." To most farmers, however, the term "cab" is more familiar.

The New Generation tractors were never available with Deere & Company manufactured cabs. By the late 1960s, cabs built by outside manufacturers were being installed both in the field and at the Deere & Company factories. However, the events that led to the development of the famous Sound-Gard cab began during the New Generation era.

Cabs were envisioned and tried on tractors as early as 1912. Back then the Heer

Engine Company of Portsmouth, Ohio, featured a factory cab with side curtains much like a buggy. In 1921, cabs were even standard equipment on the Savage tractor manufactured by the Savage Harvester Company of Denver, Colorado.

Many of these early attempts at protecting the tractor operator were crude and ineffective.

Considering the noise level of early tractors, the dusty conditions in working ground or harvesting crops, all coupled with the lack of air conditioning, meant that the cab concept was years ahead of its time. Tractor operators realized the best device was an umbrella or open canopy that protected them from the sun and rain yet let the breeze keep the driver cool and clear away the dust.

The 1938 Minneapolis-Moline U-DLX Comfortractor sported the most advanced cab of its time. The unit was equipped with a radio, heater, and windshield wipers. It, too, wasn't advanced enough, or perhaps it was too advanced, to capture the imagination and pocketbooks of farmers. Only approximately 150 of these intriguing units were sold.

There the concept languished until 1960 when Deere & Company and other tractor manufacturers noticed that aftermarket companies were beginning to sell cab units that could be successfully fitted to their tractors.

The story of the development of the now famous Deere & Company cab is told by one of the men who did pioneering work on the project, retired Deere engineer Harold Brock.

Brock recalled when one of the Deere employees was killed in a rollover accident: "We realized then we needed to provide a roll guard of some type for testing, not for normal use, but for strictly testing. Testing can be hazardous when a test operator has to pick up a load and raise it all the way up and swing it around repeatedly. So, we designed a roll guard and put it on all our tractors to protect the test people operating them."

This idea developed into an extensive

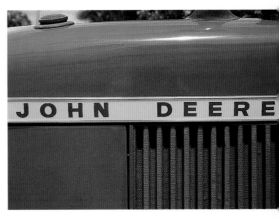

Even the "John Deere" on the tractors was changed to combine a sturdy, can-get-it-done feel with a gracefulness that bespoke speed.

testing program to develop a roll guard structure. And the company began to consider the roll guard for production. "We didn't know anything about rollover requirements at first," Brock said. "So, we bought a mannequin and strapped it on the tractor and rolled the tractor." The cab structure went through many different designs before it was finalized.

When Deere decided to offer the roll cage as a production option, Brock remembers all the competitors were invited to the Deere engineering center for a demonstration. Deere was recommending that all tractors include this safety feature and was willing to share its design and test data.

This design greatly influenced the safety aspect of the entire agricultural machinery industry. Tractors are often operated on hills and inclines, making them susceptible to rollover. High-clearance tractors also have a tendency to roll more than do utility models.

Brock said that led to a company decision to build a cab for tractors. "Customers were buying aftermarket cabs and installing them on the old Wheat Belt tractors," Brock recalled. "These cabs weren't satisfactory, because they were noisy and hot. They didn't have air conditioning, so we said we should design a cab that's air conditioned."

At this time, Deere was buying cabs from outside sources and installing them on

The 1010 Crawler is quite easy to operate. Note the combination tachometer-speedometer. The gearshift is located on the transmission.

tractors destined for the Wheat Belt. Brock thought it was a better idea to design a John Deere-specific cab, one that couldn't be converted to use on a competitor's tractor. "It would be like a car body," Brock said.

The first point to address was to design it as a pod, in other words, isolated from the vehicle. "All the other cabs that were being produced were so noisy due to excessive vibration. All that noise was coming right off the steering wheel and frame," Brock said. "Our goal was to isolate the cab and make it quiet, and to air condition it, both of which we did."

The success in reducing noise resulted from Brock calling on some of his friends in the auto business. "When it got to noise, nobody in the ag machinery industry knew

anything about reducing sound in movable vehicles. I called my friends at General Motors, Ford, and Chrysler, and asked them what they did to reduce sound in their car bodies. They replied, 'Well, nobody has a formula for this. We do it by the seat of the pants by trying different things.'

"Then people at the GMC research center told me there was a man in New York who was a good acoustical man on buildings, and that we might want to have him come advise us. We picked his brain on what he knew about buildings. From this we knew better how to mount the cab on a tractor to isolate it and remove more noise. We eventually got the inside sound down to as low as that of a passenger car."

A consideration was given to have the cabs produced by A. O. Smith, the company that made Chevrolet Corvette bodies. Brock suggested this would be foolish and that Deere should make the cab, however. "We were going to be the first in the industry to have a cab that's both comfortable and quiet. And I feared we were going to give this knowledge away to all our competitors," Brock said. "Besides this adds 25 percent more parts to the manufacturing process, which has potential for 25 percent more profit. And, that's what we did.

"Next we asked Lyle Cherry, in charge of the marketing group, 'How many cabs do you think you can sell?' This cab is going to be a deluxe, quiet cab with good air conditioning. The old cabs that are being put on tractors out there are unsatisfactory—and we intend to sell our cabs at approximately the same price.

"Because the market for cabs at that time was essentially Wheat Belt farmers, with almost none on row-crop tractors, marketing determined that 15 percent of our tractors should be cab-equipped. So the factory tooled up for 15 percent. That turned out to be a mistake because buyers wanted the cab on 50 percent of the new tractor orders, and that quickly rose to 75 percent. The factory had to retool to keep up with demand," Brock said.

"Do farmers realize there's never been one single person hurt who's been using a

Deere-designed cab on his tractor?"

Brock recalled an incident involving a truck driver with a cab-equipped tractor on his truck's trailer. The truck and trailer went off the highway and ended up in the ditch with the trailer on top of the cab. "The cab wasn't as squashed as you'd think it would be—it held up the trailer!" Just how good was this revolutionary cab? It was so good, that it caused Deere & Company an unusual problem. Retired PEC Director Michael Mack remembered that once the new Sound-Gard body, or cab, was introduced and marketed worldwide, dealers and farmers began calling and demanding to know why the seat had been changed. The phones were constantly ringing with complaints.

They complained that the tractor was now quite uncomfortable. Not only that, they wanted the old seat back. Deere & Company engineers were baffled, since they hadn't changed one thing concerning the seat.

As Brock pointed out, the engineers had consulted with the automobile and building industries to learn about sound control and how to make the cab as quiet as possible.

The entire unit was mounted on four rubber biscuits to insulate it from noise transmitted through the frame of the tractor. This, plus other engineering features, reduced the noise level to equal the interior noise of an automobile. But why was the tractor now so uncomfortable to operate? Once again Deere & Company sought outside professional assistance, this time consulting with an industrial psychologist. What unfolded was certainly new territory for agricultural tractor engineers.

The industrial psychologist explained that General Motors engineers had once installed a special dial on the dash of an automobile. This dial could be turned to either increase or decrease the noise level inside the car. However, the people who were asked to drive the car thought the dial adjusted seat comfort. They were asked to adjust the dial until they were the most comfortable, and what they didn't know was that the dial had absolutely nothing to do with the seat. Instead, the dial controlled only the noise level inside the car.

As the drivers motored along adjusting the dial for what they thought was optimum riding comfort, they almost invariably adjusted the dial to a higher noise level. What was this telling the engineers?

The answer, strange as it may seem: The human hearing system is one of the most complex in the body. As the noise level increases, the audio sensory system demands more and more of the operator's attention than do the nerve endings in his posterior.

Translated to the situation with the new Sound-Gard body: As the noise level dropped in the new cab, operators responded to sensory input from the area of their tailbones instead of their ears.

Armed with this information, Deere & Company could have reduced the effectiveness of the state-of-the-art cab-noise-reducing ability. Instead, the company decided to wait for operators to adjust to the new unit, which they did.

The air conditioning aspect created some interesting engineering challenges as well. "A tractor cab requires twice as much air conditioning capacity as an automobile due to the large amount of glass," Brock said. "The only good air conditioning compressor made at that time was a Frigidaire, made by GM; but they didn't want to sell the rights to any outside manufacturers. The aftermarket cabs used a reciprocating piston-type compressor that was ugly and set way up on the engine." Deere didn't want that.

Through a contact Brock had with Frigidaire, he was able to get an agreement to purchase the units, with the stipulation that nothing be altered in their design.

"We put them on tractors and began testing right away," Brock said. "The confounded things lasted only 200 hours or so in the dust and vibration of farming, before the seals started leaking.

"So then I said to my guys: 'We've got to correct this—and not tell GM what we're doing.'" Brock secured the cooperation—

The Wheatland tractor moved on a narrower front end, had larger fenders, was designed for pulling and so didn't mount a three-point hitch, and the driver mounted from the rear rather than from the side.

Although the additional power of the 4020 was appreciated over the 4010, it came equipped with an even more appreciated advancement: Power Shift Transmission. Moving just one handy up-front lever allowed the driver to shift well-spaced gears under load and on the go, all without any clutching.

Early New Generation "10 Series" tractors had the gearshift lever located handily right on the console and convenient to the driver's right hand.

and a vow of secrecy—of the bearing seal manufacturer, and his engineering group designed a dust box and vibration, which GM had never done before.

"We finally perfected a new seal and bearing that would fit into the same space. I had to go back to my friend at GM and say, 'Well, we promised not to change it. But, we have something here that makes it so much better and doesn't cost any more money. You should really adopt it. It would be better for your cars and trucks.'"

Brock said, "It took us roughly two-and-a-half years to do it, but we came up with a good compressor, one that became a new standard for the entire industry."

Right
This 4620 Diesel was the 459th made and was delivered to the John Deere Engineering Department and not to a dealership. This tractor became a testbed for potential options, because it's "loaded." Unique for its day, it had front-wheel assist, three selective control valves (SCVs), optional lighting, quick hitch and a factory installed cab. The engine delivered whopping 135 horsepower.

3

D-DAY

The New Generation development was shrouded in deep security from the beginning, awaiting precisely the right moment to unveil seven years of determined effort. The question now became how to most effectively introduce the New Generation to the distributors, dealers, and the agri-world in general.

In the past, Deere & Company had taken its new products along with key personnel to regional sites around the country for introductions and demonstrations. Keeping with the concept of new methods of thinking, however, this time management of Deere & Company felt the need to showcase the new products on a much grander scale.

Grand could well be an understatement in this instance. Colossal might be more correct to describe the New Generation tractor's debut in Dallas, Texas. Such an ambitious concept came with a price tag of approximately $1,250,000 and two years of diligent preparation.

The effort combined the brilliantly staged choreography of a Broadway show with the logistics of a military invasion, which the press referred to as the day "Deere took Dallas."

Once the target date and location had been set, it was time to address the details of actually making it happen. What resulted was the staging of the largest exhibit of farm and industrial equipment ever displayed by a single manufacturer.

The list of the jobs that needed completing was long: housing for an anticipated 6,000 distributors, dealers, industry leaders, financiers, and Deere management and personnel; transportation for participants from all across the United States, Canada, and 19 other countries; food and drink, entertainment big and gaudy enough to uphold Texas tradition; facilities for hundreds of tractors and equipment to be properly housed and displayed; facilities to seat 6,000 people so they could hear and see the presentation of the new product; and the transporting of 136 new tractors and 223 pieces of equipment from Waterloo and Dubuque, Iowa, to Dallas, Texas, all under wraps to preserve the secret just a mite longer.

Deere personnel set aside their familiar "hats" of management, engineer, or line worker and donned new hats of travel agent, food service coordinator, and entertainment manager, plus a host of other unfamiliar roles. Many of these employees were relieved of their regular duties and for two years concentrated solely on producing the big event.

So successful were their efforts, that those involved seem to recall only a single incident of lost luggage. The only other miscalculation that Hewitt recalls was a change in travel plans for a couple that opted for ground transportation instead of an airline.

Maybe the near-perfect execution of the intensive preparation isn't all that surprising considering the painstaking plan-

In Moline, Illinois, designers and engineers used this model layout as an aid in determining how the outside exhibit area should be arranged at the Dallas introduction.

The crowd was large at the New Generation tractor introduction at the Dallas Memorial Auditorium in Texas, August 30, 1960. All roads seemed to lead to the outdoor exhibit area of New Generation tractors and related equipment.

The biggest challenge was transportation. As a result, the Deere & Company "travel agency" enlisted the assistance of a handful of United Air Lines personnel who worked side-by-side for an entire year to coordinate 16 U.S. and Canadian airlines. Private planes and charter flights rounded out the airlift.

The event was impressive enough to be written up in the September 12, 1960, issue of *Aviation Week and Space Technology,* which tabulated more than 100 scheduled and 60 charter flights. This was billed as the largest airlift of its type ever attempted.

Deere & Company personnel even donned the "hat" of a meteorologist. They checked out past Dallas weather records and consulted long-range forecasts to prevent Mother Nature from raining on Deere's parade and gala unveiling.

By nightfall August 29, 1960, Deere & Company was at last ready to raise the curtain on a new era in agricultural machinery.

It's Show Time!

The Deere & Company air armada first began touching down at Love Field, Dallas, Texas, in the early hours of August 29, 1960.

By the time the last flight touched down, 5,000 eager distributors, dealers, and guests were ready to participate in the excitement. Joining them were approximately 1,500 more that arrived by bus, railroad, and automobile.

This was to be the first time in modern Deere & Company history that the entire sales force had been gathered under one roof.

Deere & Company headquarters was established at the Statler Hilton hotel, where a press conference was held Monday afternoon. On hand to field questions was Bill Hewitt and C. R. Carlson Jr., vice president in charge of marketing.

The curiosity of the press provided some lively questioning. Yet nothing was divulged that would diminish the big surprise scheduled for the next day when the New Generation tractors would be unveiled. More than anything, the press conference

ning that hallmarked the months and months of getting ready for the big event.

At Deere & Company headquarters in Moline, Illinois, the entire exhibit was first created in miniature, from the 15-acre parking area where the machinery would be displayed to the interior of the coliseum. Using toy tractors, puppets, and models, the placement of each piece was predetermined to eliminate any surprises when it came time for the real show.

Nothing was overlooked regarding the

convenience and safety of those attending either. More than 100 charter buses traveled the routes from the airport to the 21 hotels and motels that housed the guests. Cowgirls, local cheerleaders and drill team members dressed in miniskirts and armed with placards, guided the passengers from plane to proper bus.

A first aid station with attending physicians stood by for any emergency. There was even an allergist to treat anyone who suffered from the unfamiliar Texas dust or pollens.

WHY DALLAS?

Why did Deere & Company choose Dallas, Texas, as the site for the unveiling of its new tractor line? Perhaps the reason was best verbalized by Stanley Marcus in an editorial Monday, September 5, 1960, in *The Dallas Morning News*:

"When the great Deere & Company decided to unveil its new lines of tractors and industrial equipment to its entire worldwide dealership at one time, it researched the country for the city having all the qualities it required. Dallas was chosen, because Dallas was ready.

"First of all, Deere & Company needed 6,500 first-class rooms in which to house its dealers and other guests. Dallas hotels and motels met that requirement, for Dallas has been on a hotel-building spree since the new Statler Hilton was started Oct. 7, 1953.

"Second, Deere & Company needed an air-conditioned auditorium capable of seating 6,500 guests with perfect vision for all. Also, another air-conditioned auditorium of equal size with a dirt floor on which their tractors could be operated. Finally, open ground area adjacent to the second auditorium on which their new pieces of equipment could be field-demonstrated.

"Because Dallas citizens had voted affirmatively in the bond elections of 1927 and 1945 to spend $8,000,000 for the construction of the Dallas Memorial Auditorium . . . because the State Fair of Texas had decided in 1945 to build a coliseum of proper size and dimensions to have livestock shows . . . and since the State Fair had the open fields available, Dallas met these second requirements.

"Third, since Deere & Company was going to stage the biggest private air-lift in American history, it had to have a city that had adequate landing capabilities for hundreds of planes within 24 hours, adequate repair facilities, and adequate regular transcontinental routes. The company wanted to avoid a long air-to-city haul-in for 6,500 guests, so it was looking for a city with a close-in airport.

"Since the citizens of Dallas had voted for the enlargement and expansion of Love Field in 1952, since Dallas is served by American, Braniff, Continental, Delta, Trans Texas, Central, Lone Star, since Love Field is just 20 minutes from the center of Downtown, since this city is nationally famous for its aircraft maintenance, Dallas met the specifications on all grounds.

"Fourth, Deere & Company required a variety of services ranging from a catering organization capable of feeding 6,500 guests at a single sitting to top-quality musicians capable of playing the specially scored music for the dramatic presentation of its new products. The famous Jetton organization of Fort Worth was well-able to handle the food assignment. And, because Dallas has supported a great Symphony Orchestra for so long, the company were [*sic*] able to find all of the highly skilled musicians they required.

"Fifth, the company needed good weather, and they did a research job on end-of-August weather in Dallas during the past five years. We can't exactly claim the credit, but Deere & Company got the good weather it needed.

"Deere & Company surveyed the country and found that Dallas met all its requirements better than any other city in America. Dallas was ready! And, because Dallas was ready, Dallas benefited by this great industrial air-lift that brought 6,500 John Deere distributors from all over the world to our city. They spent more than $1,000,000. This went to our hotels and motels, display companies, musicians, electricians, newspapers, auditorium and coliseum rentals, caterers, and a host of other business services."

In the vanguard of the parade that launched the New Generation tractors to the 6,500 people were some more of the Texas cowgirls who also served as guides and greeters.

whetted the appetites of those in attendance, but seeing and touching would have to wait one more day.

After the press conference, those who enjoyed VIP status attended a Deere & Company-hosted dinner at the Statler Hilton. Once again a welcoming committee of pretty Texas cowgirls was on hand to pin a yellow rose onto each guest. It was a time for company personnel to see old friends as well as rub shoulders with city officials. Bankers and the press also had the opportunity to have one-on-one conversations with Deere & Company management and to enjoy the hospitality.

It had been 131 years since John Deere started fulfilling his business dreams. He probably would've been astounded to see the growth and progress of his company and proud to see that two of his direct descendants were still actively involved with the company.

The professional ice revue that preceded the introduction was well-choreographed and got the crowd into the proper mood.

Bill Hewitt's wife, Patricia Deere Wiman, was the daughter of Charles Deere Wiman, who was the son of Anna Deere. Anna Deere was the daughter of Charles Deere, who was the son of John Deere.

Also enjoying the evening was Benjamin C. Keator, a direct descendant of John Deere, a longtime employee, and a Deere & Company board member from 1949 to 1954.

After enjoying fine food and drink, the guests retired to their hotels and motels for a few hours of rest before D-Day dawned in Dallas.

Tuesday, August 30, 1960, brought clear skies, and eventually the oppressive heat that visitors and residents of Texas don't soon forget. It wasn't long before the company's search for facilities that offered air conditioning was greatly appreciated.

However, large crowds of John Deere dealers and guests gathered outside the Dallas Memorial Auditorium to anxiously await the official starting time of 10 A.M. Those staying at hotels and motels within walking distance arrived early, while those relying on the bus brigade soon followed.

By the scheduled 10 A.M. start time, everyone had been ushered to comfortable, upholstered theater seats while the orchestra played "Dixie," "The Eyes of Texas," "California Here I Come," "Oklahoma," and "Iowa."

An ice rink had been set up on the arena floor and the festivities opened with a full-scale ice show. Skaters from the Hollywood Ice Revue performed a routine choreographed around the theme, "Welcome to Deere Day in Dallas."

After the ice show, a 10-minute film depicting the history of Deere & Company was shown via a specially built five-sided movie screen. Notwithstanding all that Dallas offered as the perfect convention center, the Memorial Auditorium didn't come complete with a five-sided movie screen suspended from its ceiling. In fact, the circular seating of the auditorium made it impossible for a single screen to be viewed from all the seats in the house.

As each new model entered, it was joined by another type of model carrying a large, easily read sign that explained what it was. In this instance, this was the 3010 Row-Crop Single Front Wheel tractor.

Deere & Company contracted with Wilding Pictures of Chicago, Illinois, to build the five-sided screen. Lightweight magnesium was used in its construction since it was to be suspended from the auditorium's roof. The screen was shipped in sections from Chicago and required a week for installation.

When the program switched from live presentation via closed circuit TV to film footage, it required five identical films be projected in perfect synchronization.

Then Hewitt made the welcoming address. Hewitt and other speakers were televised "live" onto the screens.

Then came the time for which all had labored so long, the moment of truth. The film was rolled, and the secret that Deere & Company had guarded for seven long years was revealed. For 10 short minutes, the audience was captivated by the "New Generation of Power" projected on the big screens.

The audience was intrigued, yet still had to wait just a little longer to see the new tractors and equipment "in the flesh." Immediately following the film, C. R. Carlson Jr. addressed the crowd.

Another ice review emphasizing the points in the previous film quickly followed. Then once again the big screens came to life

and showed a film dealing with the research and development of the new line of tractors. The program closed with a third ice revue with the theme, "Great days are coming."

On a lower level of the auditorium, the Walter Jetton catering service was preparing 6,500 box lunches for the visitors.

While the crowd was devouring their lunches, Hewitt and other VIPs departed for downtown Dallas and the prestigious Neiman-Marcus store. Here, at the stroke of noon, another carefully executed promotion added unprecedented "class" to the heretofore lowly farm tractor.

Both designer Dreyfuss and Hewitt

A crowd gathers in the world-famed Neiman-Marcus store in downtown Dallas—a great public relations coup—to view the new 3010 tractor on display during "D-Day." Note that the tractor "wears" a diamond bracelet atop its exhaust stack and is also festooned with other diamonds that are worth an estimated $2 million. By the tractor, from left, are Deere & Company President and CEO Bill Hewitt; Henry Dreyfuss, industrial designer; Stanley Marcus, Neiman-Marcus; and Hewitt's wife, Patricia Deere Wiman, a descendent of John Deere through her father, former Deere & Company President and CEO Charles D. Wiman.

were friends of Stanley Marcus, president of Neiman-Marcus Company. From this trio came the idea to display a New Generation tractor inside the prestigious Neiman-Marcus department store.

The tractor was positioned on the first floor, directly across from the store's exclusive jewelry display. A large panel arranged like a 20-foot gift box tied with a huge ribbon added suspense and secrecy until the big moment.

With fanfare and expectation the ribbon was cut and the wrapping removed to reveal a shining 3010 Diesel Row-Crop, complete with the ever-present smiling Texas cowgirl.

The effect was stunning—especially considering that a diamond coronet

adorned the exhaust stack and other diamond jewelry was taped on the hood spelling out "John Deere." When questioned about the value of the gems, Hewitt estimated the jewelry amounted to, "a couple million dollars worth."

Hewitt smiled when recalling the bizarre problem the company encountered getting the tractor into the Neiman-Marcus store, although it seemed less humorous back then.

When the tractor showed up at the department store, it was discovered the building didn't have a door large enough to allow the big tractor to enter. A crew of workers descended on the store in the early hours that morning. They came in with a "nothing is impossible" attitude that hallmarks all great achievements.

Working under floodlights at 2 A.M., they removed store-front windows that were several feet above the sidewalk. Next, a ramp was constructed from the street up to the window opening. Now the task was as simple as firing up the 3010 and driving it up the ramp and into the store.

Once inside the engine was turned off, and the tractor was manually pushed to the desired location.

Following the lunch at Memorial Auditorium, the guests were bussed to the Texas State Fairgrounds. Inside the Livestock Coliseum, they saw real New Generation tractors for the first time. Every model was paraded through the arena with cowgirls carrying signs identifying each model. The show was greeted with cheers and applause until the last tractor rolled past in review.

Finally it was time to open the coliseum doors and let the anxious crowd of 6,500 move out into the outdoor exhibit area to see, touch, and examine the goods. It contained fifteen acres of goods, 136 new tractors, and 223 implements—almost the entire Deere & Company agricultural and industrial lines.

The extent of the display and the hospitable surroundings was impressive. It sparked the press to churn out millions of words of copy expounding the merits of D-Day in Dallas and the industry-leading features of the new products.

But the show wasn't over yet. There were more "goods" to come. Some of these could be sampled at what was billed, "the longest bar in Texas, or anywhere else." It was set up at the edge of the machinery exhibit where willing guests could slake their thirst in real Texas style.

People could even take their shots of "red-eye" and stroll down the streets of a recreated frontier town and view a livery stable, saloon, Wells Fargo office, bank, "Boothill Monument Company," and a replica of John Deere's blacksmith shop. Freeman Decorating Company's Helen Anderson painted portraits of historical

The array of diamonds sported by this new 3010 on display in the Neiman-Marcus store in downtown Dallas on "D-Day" is worth an estimated $2 million. Note that diamonds spell out "John Deere" on the hood, while there's a diamond bracelet on top of the exhaust stack. From left, are Deere & Company President and CEO Bill Hewitt; Henry Dreyfuss, industrial designer; Stanley Marcus, Neiman-Marcus; and Hewitt's wife, Patricia Deere Wiman.

figures including Doc Holliday, Wyatt Earp, and Johnny Ringo.

But there was more. When chow time rolled around, it was a culinary event large enough for both the occasion and crowd. Walter Jetton, king of the Texas barbecue caterers, had been working behind the scenes to unveil his own spectacular show.

He had to plan a barbecue for 6,500 guests that included 1,000 tables and 6,500 chairs to seat the guests, 5,000 pounds of beef (including whole beefs roasted over open pits), 1,800 pounds of ribs, 4,200 chickens, 300 gallons of ranch beans, 2,500 pounds of potato salad, 6,000 ears of corn, 1,500 pounds of Texas coleslaw, 15,000 sourdough biscuits, 7,500 apple turnovers, 300 pounds of butter, 10 barrels of iced tea, and 200 gallons of steaming coffee.

By 8:30 P.M. the well-fed and watered crowd moved into the nearby Cotton Bowl for the grand finale. The fireworks display brought round after round of "oohs" and "ahs" and applause as the John Deere emblem, tractor outlines, and "New Generation of Power" motifs were created by fireworks exploding high against the Texas night sky.

With one last crescendo of bursting sound and color, Deere Day in Dallas became history.

A newspaper reporter wrote, " Factory men fielded questions at Dallas, but no attempt was made to take orders and no hint was given as to prices of the new tractors and equipment."

After the fireworks had faded into the Texas night and the last flight had departed Love Field, the next step was to sell the product with all the effort that had been devoted to developing the line of New Generation tractors.

THE 1000 SERIES

The various New Generation model numbers, 1010, 2010, and so on, have often evoked curiosity in farmers and restorers as to their origin. Over the years, some tractor model numbers, for example, indicate the PTO horsepower, the drawbar horsepower, or both. In other instances the model numbers simply identified the year the tractor was introduced. Others seemingly follow no logic.

"We already had all these different designations," Hewitt said. "There was a Model A, a Model B, no Model C, a Model D, but no E, F, or G. There was a GP and an LA, and then finally we skipped all the way up to the Model R.

"There was absolutely no rhyme nor reason for the sequence of alphabetical letters we were using. That bothered me. So I said, 'Look, we're coming out with a completely new set of models and an assortment of horsepower size capabilities. Let's designate them in some logical sequence.'

"I don't know exactly who came up with the 1010, 2010, 3010, 4010, and so forth. But, instead of 1, 2, 3, or 4, it was better to have four numerals. You can have four numerals and easily say them in two words. If it's a 1-0-1-0, you can call it a 'Ten-ten.' If its a 4-0-1-0, that's 'Forty-ten.' "

Although many farmers and restorers refer to the "3010 Series" or "4020 Series" tractors, according to Deere & Company officials that nomenclature doesn't reflect the original definition. Instead, they differentiate the New Generation tractors as the "10 Series" (for instance, 1010, 2010, 3010, and 4010), and the "20 Series" (as in 1020, 2020, 3020, and 4020).

Retired director of the product engineering center Harold Brock, recalled some corporate worries with regard to the new tractors. "We had concerns with the 3010 and 4010, whether the farmers were going to accept a high-speed engine, not to mention whether they'd accept higher horsepower to run faster with their implements.

"As it turned out, they loved these tractors and the engine speed of 2,000-plus rpm rather than the chug-chug-chug of the two-cylinder's approximately 975 rpm.

"Incidentally, piston speed in the New Generation engine was no faster than it was in the old two-cylinder engine. I'm talking here about velocity of the piston, which was no greater than on the old, slower speed engine. So, the farmer really wasn't going to wear the new engine out any faster. "

1010 Models 1961–1965

This was the smallest New Generation tractor introduced at Deere Day. Four models were originally offered: Utility, Row-Crop Utility, Single Row-Crop, and Crawler. These tractors were made at the Dubuque, Iowa, facility and were an important part of the line until 1965.

Sales literature described the 1010

This industrial 1010 is a stripped-down model that lacks power steering and a three-point hitch. It came from the factory painted bright orange to enhance the safety of township employees operating it. When new in 1963, it cost $3,160. Weight was 3,923 pounds, and the PTO horsepower was rated at 36.

This early 1010 Utility has the gearshift lever for the five-speed transmission on the console. It's one of only a few 1010s equipped with optional power steering. In common with other tractors made at the Dubuque, Iowa, plant, the clutch has a tendency to stick if the tractor sits for a long period of time. John Deere touted the less-than-shoulder height of the hood line, actually 50 inches, of this tractor.

models as "compact" tractors able to provide "a man's work at a boy's pay." At 35 horsepower, the 1010 fit into Deere & Company's line-up with just a little more horsepower than the previous 430 model and just a tad less horsepower than the 530.

The 1010 was essentially a 430 with a new engine and styling to match the New Generation appearance. Much of the tractor was manufactured using the existing tooling that had produced the 430 tractor.

All 1010 models have a variable-speed four-cylinder gasoline or diesel engine. The four-cylinder engines incorporated two counter-rotating balance shafts that reduced the vibration inherent in four-cylin-

der engines. Deere & Company engines were alone in providing this concept for smoother-running four-bangers.

All wheeled models have a five-speed sliding-gear transmission. The crawler has a four-speed sliding-gear transmission. Notable differences between these tractors and the new engineering on the 3010 and 4010 include the hydraulic system, transmission, and engine.

These 1010 engines feature a sleeve-and-deck design allowing all four-cylinder sleeves to be combined into one unit. According to retired engineer Jack Decker, who worked on the design of the sleeve and deck engines, this design was used on the three- and four-cylinder engines, and was discontinued around 1965.

Sleeve and deck engines were manufactured at Dubuque and used in the lower horsepower tractors. Decker worked at the PEC in Waterloo, but traveled back and forth to Dubuque as his services were required.

According to Decker, "The gasoline version was a pretty good engine, although the diesel was a little on the weak side, though. The whole philosophy behind the sleeve and deck was to get a larger engine without having to design a whole new set of patterns and molds for the foundry."

One of the difficulties with the design involved attaching the sleeves to the deck. The deck was counterbored and the sleeves were flared on the end that interfaced with the deck. Welding material was placed between the counterbored and the sleeve flange. This was done cold.

Then the unit was placed in an oven that heated the metal to a temperature which welded the sleeve to the deck. The deck would tend to warp during this process of heating and cooling, causing some alignment concerns.

The bottom of the block had a counterbore to accept the sleeves when the sleeve and deck were assembled to the block. O-rings were installed to provide a seal at the bottom of the cylinder sleeves. Any warpage in the deck caused slight misalignment of the sleeves and bottom O-rings and could result in coolant or oil getting into the cylinder. These problems were eliminated on the gasoline engine once the oven-welding process was corrected.

The higher heat and higher compression of the diesel engine contributed to the failure of the seals of the O-rings on the diesel models.

On later model 1010 tractors, the gear shift was relocated downward directly over the transmission.

Next
Here are two 1010 Single Row-Crops, a slighter more narrow, taller tractor that replaced the 430 Standard. The left "twin" is a partially restored gas model, while the one at right is the diesel model. It features several options including power steering, independent dual speed 540-rpm and 1,000-rpm PTOs, and dual rear rockshaft and one remote cylinder hydraulic system. There were many different front ends available for the various 1010s. One even included an offset seat and chassis arrangement that gave the driver a clearer view down the right side of the tractor. The others were adjustable straight axle, adjustable swept-back axle, single wheel, and Roll-O-Matic dual front wheels.

This 1010 Single Row-Crop exited the Dubuque, Iowa, factory with a full load of goodies: power steering, independent dual speed 540-rpm and 1,000-rpm PTOs, and dual rear rockshaft and one remote cylinder hydraulic system. It's rated at up to 35 horsepower at maximum rpm measured at the PTO.

The front end of this 1010 intended for row-crop usage runs on Roll-O-Matic dual front wheels.

On the new Waterloo tractors, the fuel tank was moved to the front of the tractor, while the Dubuque models retained the standard location over the engine.

An economical version of the 1010, known as the Special Row-Crop Utility, could be ordered with pan seat, 540-rpm PTO, and five-speed transmission.

The 1010 also offered the rarest New Generation tractor of all—a single Hi-Crop model was built.

Eventually the 1010 was manufactured in 10 variations. Model names and alpha codes are:

Single Row-Crop Tractor (RS)
Row-Crop Tractor (R)
Row-Crop Utility Tractor (RU)
Utility Tractor (U)
Special Row-Crop Utility Tractor (RUS)
Grove and Orchard Tractor (O)
Hi-Crop Tractor (H)
Agricultural Crawler Tractor (CA)
Industrial Crawler (C)
Industrial Wheel Tractor (W)

(Alpha code refers to the function or type of vehicle. The production code was a manufacturing process designation.)

1010 Single-Row Crop Tractor

Design of this 1010 was aimed specifically for working single rows of specialty crops such as tobacco or vegetables. Offset front wheels and a seat that could be offset offered the operator a great view of the single row being worked.

This unit was also available with two independently controlled rear rockshafts and a three-point hitch with Load-and-Depth Control sensing.

1010 Row-Crop Utility Tractor

Even with its low profile, this 1010 had good under-axle clearance of 20 inches for cultivating standing crops. Its low profile, coupled with available swept-back front axle, provided a shorter wheelbase that made it especially handy for working inside buildings or cleaning pens.

This unit was available with two independently controlled rear rockshafts and a three-point hitch with Load-and-Depth

Destined to be a dedicated mower all its days, this industrial 1010 carried a bright yellow paint color. Although the tractor didn't come with a three-point hitch, it has a hydraulic pump mounted on the front of the crankshaft so it can drive the mower and raise and lower it.

More agricultural 1010 Crawlers were equipped with three-point hitches than were the similar industrial models. The most common configuration was a front-mounted blade or bucket with a rear drawbar-type hitch.

Control sensing, plus adjustable front axle. It was powered by either a gasoline or diesel engine and was available with manual or power steering.

1010 Utility Tractor

This model was billed as an extra-low tractor for working in vineyards, groves, and orchards. It was particularly handy on smaller farms where its chores included tillage, haying, loading, and hauling.

It could be taken home to the farm with choices of gasoline or diesel engine, manual or power steering, regular or deluxe seat, vertical or horizontal muffler, underneath exhaust, manually adjusted or power-adjusted rear wheels.

1010 Grove and Orchard Tractor

The Grove and Orchard Tractor was added to the New Generation line-up in 1962. The utility model was the basis of this tractor. Its features included underslung exhaust, low-mounted headlights, side shield, and wide fenders.

It was outfitted to protect both the trees and the operator when working in groves and orchards. It could be ordered with the full range of options available for the 1010 tractors.

1010 Agricultural Crawler Tractor

A multipurpose track-laying machine, this 1010 readily found a market in farming areas that required the flotation or stability capabilities of the crawler-type tractor. It was also capable of dozing, excavating, and handling many other kinds of industrial jobs.

It was available as a "loaded" version with platform and fenders, heavy-duty front bottom plate, four-speed transmission, exhaust muffler cover (diesel), rock guards (five-roller), track-tension adjuster (manual), gasoline or diesel engine, four- or five-roller track assembly, or four-roller with oversize front idler, and choice of type and size track shoes.

These twin levers control the dual Touch-O-Matic hydraulic system for the "10 Series" tractors. The driver had the choice of, say when cultivating, moving just one lever down to drop one side of the cultivator or pushing both down to lower both sides of the cultivator.

Note: The production breakdown information for the 1010 (below)—and similar information for all the subsequent series that follow—is provided by and used with the permission of Jack Cherry, courtesy of the Two-Cylinder Club and its official publication, *Two-Cylinder*.

Although every effort has been made to provide the most accurate data possible, neither Cherry nor the authors can guarantee 100 percent accuracy. No factory production log is known to exist. So the numbers were arrived at by individually examining each entry in the serial number register.

1010 Production

Prod. Year*	Single Row-Crop		Row-Crop		Row-Crop Utility		Utility	
	Gas	Diesel	Gas	Diesel	Gas	Diesel	Gas	Diesel
1960	201	81	0	0	0	0	88	9
1961	1,157	307	0	0	1,926	11	503	169
1962	897	52	0	0	1,501	423	380	65
1963	990	125	592	57	1,269	543	421	30
1964	740	62	532	104	1,380	431	431	46
1965**	582	60	368	112	972	536	287	34
Total	4,567	687	1,492	273	7,048	2,744	2,110	353

Prod. Year*	Special Row-Crop Utility		Agricultural Orchard		Hi-Crop Crawler	
	Gas	Gas	Diesel	Gas	Gas	Diesel
1960	0	0	0	0	135	2
1961	0	0	0	0	71	68
1962	200	33	5	0	75	34
1963	2,753	17	0	1	48	14
1964	1,253	10	2	0	49	9
1965**	732	3	2	0	2	0
Total	4,938	63	9	1	380	127

Prod. Year*	Industrial Crawler		Industrial Wheel	
	Gas	Diesel	Gas	Diesel
1960	1,921	1,246	8	0
1961	2,068	1,715	840	362
1962	1,702	1,422	400	185
1963	1,527	1,002	452	181
1964	1,713	1,262	392	191
1965**	113	62	540	232
Total	9,094	6,709	2,632	1,151

* Normal production years began November 1 and ended October 31, or the week ending nearest that date. Model years began following the midsummer annual inventory and maintenance shutdown. As a result, tractors built in 1960 are 1961 models; those built from August to December 1961 are 1962 models.
** Production of 1010 models ceased in September 1965.

Production code information wasn't included on the serial number plate. Serial number plates are located on the right side of the engine block. A production code wasn't assigned to the Hi-Crop, as only one was built. These are the codes for each of the nine model types:

AA = Agricultural Crawler
AB = Industrial Crawler
AC = Single Row-Crop
AD = Row-Crop Utility
AE = Row-Crop

AG = Industrial Wheel
AH = Utility
AJ = Orchard
AK = Special Row-Crop Utility

This is a completely restored 1010 Crawler. In addition to being probably the only completely restored 1010 Crawler, this tractor has several other claims to uniqueness: It's a gas-powered agricultural tractor with a three-point hitch. Although John Deere built 16,310 1010 Crawler tractors, just 507 carried the green paint of agricultural tractors. All the rest were industrial tractors. Of the 507 agricultural 1010 Crawlers manufactured, only 380 were gas. Finally, most 1010 Crawlers were fitted with blades or scoops and drawbars in the rear than a three-point hitch operated by two hydraulic cylinders.

The Model 1010 was powered by gas or diesel engines and was available with a long list of options, including manual or power steering, regular or deluxe seat, vertical or horizontal muffler, underneath exhaust, manually adjusted or power adjusted wheels.

1020 1965–1973

With the introduction of the 20 series, a three-cylinder gasoline or diesel engine replaced the previous four-cylinder engine. It was the first utility tractor with closed-center hydraulics, three-point hitch with lower-link sensing, and planetary final drive. The eight-speed transmission offered four gears in both high and low ranges. Low range also provided four reverse gears.

A two-stage foot clutch allowed the PTO to continue running while the tractor's forward motion was stopped when depressing the foot clutch halfway. This proved to be a great advantage when using PTO equipment in heavy crops.

The 1020 and 2020 were the first Deere & Company tractors designed with the worldwide tractor concept in mind. Harold Brock, retired Deere & Company director of the product engineering center, headed the worldwide project.

"The worldwide tractor project started with the 20 Series tractor," Brock said.

"When we got through with the design, both the Dubuque and Mannheim, Germany, plants could use the same set of tooling."

According to Brock, the project took three years to complete. He outlined it in a series of steps: First, establish the tractor specifications; second, the cost of manufacturing had to be reduced 25 percent from the current tractors, because current manufacturing expenses were too high compared to the main competition. At the same time, the tractor had to include all the features farmers needed.

"We had to go through many, many design concepts in order to have the tractor meet its objectives," Brock said. "I gave each of the engineers a budget, saying, 'Here's your engine and this is what it's going to cost. Here's your sheet metal, your styling, your axle, your transmission.'

"I told them, 'When we have a design that meets that budget, then we're ready to go.' But that took a lot of detailed study.

Anyone can reduce costs; however, to make the product better at the same time was our real objective."

The tractors turned out to be much better than anticipated. They had many of the same features as the 3020 and 4020, such as, engine, hydraulics, transmission, and operation concepts.

Of greater note was the fact that these tractors were much better than the products previously produced at these two factories, and part of the economy was that a number of parts were interchangeable between the 1020 and the 2020. This reduced the total number of parts that needed to be produced by approximately 35 percent.

"We took that same drafting practice," Brock said, "and applied it to our future row-crop tractors. Eventually, all of Deere & Company's products were converted to worldwide designs in even metrics and the odd decimals."

With the upgrade from the 1010 to the 1020, the Dubuque tractor now fully

The Furrow magazine back cover ad talks about increasing the farmer's earning power, a subject certain to hit home. It also points out that there's a New Generation tractor to suit all farming needs, while illustrating a 1010 at work.

One indication of how much importance John Deere put on the smallest of the New Generation tractors, the 1010, is the attractive, thick, color brochure of which this is the cover page. The contents of several 1010-oriented brochures appear on pages 62 and 63. Of course, many of the features described and illustrated apply to all the New Generation tractors.

reflected the New Generation concept originally introduced with the 3010 and 4010. The transmission was changed to the eight-speed collar-shift transmission with four gears in a high and a low range and four reverse speeds in the low range.

All models and styles featured wide front ends. Roll-Gard with seat belt and canopy top for Roll-Gard were offered to buyers.

The fuel tank was moved to the front of the tractor. This design "advancement" moved the fuel tank to the same front location as it had been on the Waterloo Boy tractors.

The 1020 was offered in these models:
1020 Low Utility Tractor (LU)
1020 Row-Crop Utility Tractor (RU)
1020 High Utility Tractor (HU)
1020 Grove Tractor with shielded
    fenders and low profile
1020 Hi-Crop Tractor

1520 1968–1973

Many farmers on midsize to small farms wanted the upgraded features of a utility tractor to fit their needs. Dubuque responded with this 46-horsepower utility tractor. It could handle a variety of farm chores, from plowing to haying.

Proud of its new four-cylinder engine, the next two pages key in on what makes it different and better-suited for the farmer. The facing page highlights why the tractor is superior to its competition: lugging power, fast transport, and light field work combining speed with economy.

New variable-speed Diesel and gasoline engines
Deliver "years ahead" performance

New Generation 4-cylinder variable-speed (600-2500 rpm) engines blend traditional John Deere advantages—dependability, durability, performance, and value—with fresh new design for smoother, more controllable power. The result is more efficiency and higher work output in both Diesel or gasoline engines. They are designed to serve John Deere customers better.

The "1010" valve-in-head 4-cycle type gasoline engine has a bore and stroke of 3-1/2 x 3 inches; the Diesel, 3-5/8 x 3-1/2. Displacement in cubic inches is 115 for gasoline, 145 for Diesel; compression ratio, 7.6 to 1 for gasoline, 19 to 1 for Diesel.

New sleeve-and-deck design combines all four cylinder sleeves in one insert unit. The result is extreme compactness and extra-good heat dissipation; extra-easy cleaning of the water system, and speedy overhaul are made possible.

Massive, counterbalanced, drop-forged, and induction-hardened steel crankshafts are precision machined, statically and dynamically balanced for long, smooth performance. Full pressure lubrication insures an abundant flow of oil to lubricate all moving parts of the engine.

On Diesel engines, a rotor-type pump combines pumping and governing actions in one compact sealed unit; precisely meters equal amounts of fuel to each cylinder.

The cutaway Diesel engine, below, is pictured on a demonstration stand.

Masterpiece of engine design

Here are a few of the outstanding features of the "1010" Diesel engine:

1. Glow plugs for easy starting
2. Swirl cups for efficient combustion
3. Turbulence chamber; fuel injector
4. Double fuel filters
5. Aluminum alloy pistons for durability and efficient heat dissipation
6. Crankshaft located high for rigidity; has 5 main bearings
7. Replaceable precision bearing inserts
8. Chrome-plated top piston ring
9. Efficient engine ventilator
10. Pump for full-pressure lubrication

Big lugging power

The "1010" Utility Tractor with gasoline engine is pictured above as it turns out a fast, high-quality tillage job with a 475 Two-Disk Integral Plow. Both Diesel and gasoline engines deliver up to 35 PTO horsepower with excellent efficiency for lugging big tools under tough conditions.

Fast transport

Hurry to and from the field at nearly 15 mph. Here's the single Row-Crop with a KBY Disk Harrow.

Light field work

With engine throttled down, a "1010" pulls light loads, such as a 31 Sprayer, with great economy.

8

The important PTO features are covered in the following two pages of the brochure. Along with detail shots, probably the one of greatest impact on the farmer is the left-side clutch that enables the PTO to be started or stopped at any time.

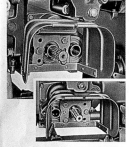

Live, independent, dual-speed power take-off
Power for today's and tomorrow's PTO machines

With live, completely independent, dual-speed power take-off—the "1010" opens the way for you to handle either 540 or the new 1000 rpm equipment, now coming into agriculture with new, more efficient machines. With this dual-speed PTO, available on Single Row-Crop and Utility models, the tractor may be started or stopped, the transmission shifted, or hydraulic system used without affecting PTO operation.

Change speeds in a hurry

This power take-off assembly includes splined outlets for a reversible stub shaft, to provide both speeds, as shown in photos at the left. The 1000 rpm outlet is at the left (top photo), and the 540 outlet is inset below. Changing from one speed to the other takes but a few minutes. A master shield and PTO guard are provided.

Choice of 5 ground speeds

The dual-speed PTO meets ASAE-SAE standards. The 540 or 1000 rpm speed is attained when the engine turns at 1900 rpm. The transmission provides five different ground speeds for PTO operation, assuring a speed that's correct for any crop or PTO machine. The speed-hour meter gives you an exact check of PTO speed at a glance.

Transmission-driven PTO

Regular equipment on the "1010" Series Tractors is an internal transmission-driven 540 rpm powershaft. A splined stub shaft may be easily attached to provide an efficient power take-off (photo at left).

Above: The stub shaft of the PTO is in 1000 rpm position (top) and 540 position (lower photo).

Below: The 540 rpm transmission-driven PTO is pictured on the John Deere "1010" Utility.

The 127 Gyramor is one of many PTO tools which work with excellent efficiency on the "1010."

Start or stop PTO any time

Here's a feature you're sure to like for its safety and convenience on a "1010" with the live, independent dual-speed PTO. A handy clutch lever, at the left side of the seat, positively and instantly engages or disengages the PTO at any time. If an implement starts to load up, tractor travel may be stopped while the machine clears itself. The PTO is stopped only by moving the lever to the rear. A safety factor permits the clutch to slip in case of a sudden overload; this prevents damage to equipment, but does not occur in normal operation.

11

Fingertip control of the hydraulic system's three-point hitch is covered in the next two pages of the brochure. The Utility model featured a single lift, while the Single Row-Crop allowed either a single or dual system.

Hydraulic System

Your touch becomes GIANT POWER for fast, easy, accurate work

Combining great lifting force with smooth and easy control, the hydraulic system of a "1010" carries out every assignment with speed and precision. You'll raise, lower, or accurately position practically all types of drawn, 3-point, and mounted equipment with an easy touch on the hydraulic lever at the right side of the seat.

In addition, the dependable gear-type hydraulic pump provides abundant capacity for exclusive Load-and-Depth Control. And, if you choose a "1010" with power steering, an extra-large capacity pump assures you of abundant hydraulic force to handle all jobs, including steering—fast, smoothly, and efficiently.

On the Utility model, a single hydraulic lift is available; for the Single Row-Crop, you can have either a single or dual system. A remote cylinder attachment is available for both "1010" Tractors.

The dual hydraulic system provides two independently controlled rear rockshafts, so you can have independent control of front- and rear-mounted equipment, and selective lift of cultivator rigs. For maximum lifting capacity, lift arms of the dual rockshaft may be locked together and lifting force of both cylinders combined. The right-hand lever then controls the rockshaft.

With either system, the rockshaft is position responsive. Working position of an implement is always in direct relation to the position of the control lever. A stop on the quadrant may be set at a selected working depth; it is easily bypassed to obtain additional working depth.

Above: The single hydraulic lever on a "1010" Single Row-Crop. The thumbscrew adjusts a stop which determines working depth of a tool; it is easily bypassed.

Left: Two hydraulic levers control a dual system available for the Single Row-Crop. Right: The powerful hydraulic pump as installed at rear of the engine.

Finger-tip control of remote cylinder and mounted tools

The versatile "1010" hydraulic system may be adapted for easy-working control of a double-acting remote cylinder (below) for operating such equipment as corn pickers, drawn plows, mowers, etc. Provision is also made for operating mounted equipment such as the 35 Loader pictured at right.

Above: The dual hydraulic system permits raising front cultivator rigs independently of the rear rig on a "1010" Single Row-Crop Tractor.

Below: The hydraulic system of a "1010" Utility goes to work operating the 35 Loader.

12

Although the three-point hydraulic system developed by Harry Ferguson for the Ford-Ferguson tractors had pioneered the three-point hitch concept several decades earlier, the idea was still new enough that two pages of the brochure were used to explain the 1010's setup and its many advantages.

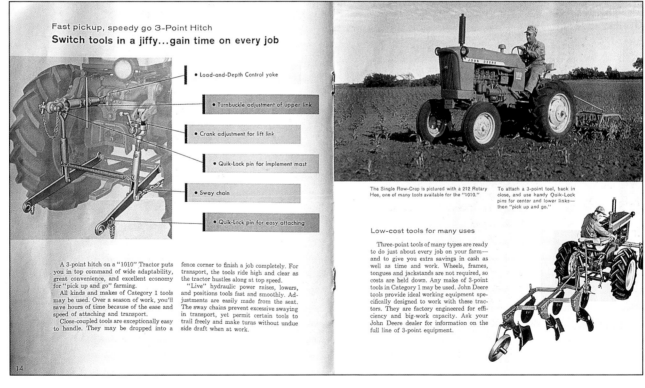

Fast pickup, speedy go 3-Point Hitch

Switch tools in a jiffy...gain time on every job

- Load-and-Depth Control yoke
- Turnbuckle adjustment of upper link
- Crank adjustment for lift link
- Quik-Lock pin for implement mast
- Sway chain
- Quik-Lock pin for easy attaching

A 3-point hitch on a "1010" Tractor puts you in top command of wide adaptability, great convenience, and excellent economy for "pick up and go" farming.

All kinds and makes of Category 1 tools may be used. Over a season of work, you'll save hours of time because of the ease and speed of attaching and transport.

Close-coupled tools are exceptionally easy to handle. They may be dropped into a fence corner to finish a job completely. For transport, the tools ride high and clear as the tractor hustles along at top speed.

"Live" hydraulic power raises, lowers, and positions tools fast and smoothly. Adjustments are easily made from the seat. The sway chains prevent excessive swaying in transport, yet permit certain tools to trail freely and make turns without undue side draft when at work.

The Single Row-Crop is pictured with a 212 Rotary Hoe, one of many tools available for the "1010."

To attach a 3-point tool, back in close, and use handy Quik-Lock pins for center and lower links—then "pick up and go."

Low-cost tools for many uses

Three-point tools of many types are ready to do just about every job on your farm—and to give you extra savings in cash as well as time and work. Wheels, frames, tongues and jackstands are not required, so costs are held down. Any make of 3-point tools in Category 1 may be used. John Deere tools provide ideal working equipment specifically designed to work with these tractors. They are factory engineered for efficiency and big-work capacity. Ask your John Deere dealer for information on the full line of 3-point equipment.

14

THE 2000 SERIES

Today, the array of available tractor models offered by each manufacturer is almost overwhelming. However, not so many years ago when you were shopping for a tractor, the local dealer offered three, four, or maybe, a half-dozen models at best. Why so many now? Who decides what models are needed in the line?

Michael Mack, retired Deere & Company director of the product engineering center, explained that it all starts with the customer. The engineering group and the marketing group work in tandem to put their fingers on the pulse of the customers and their needs. They have to establish some sort of product definition, and this is quite different in various parts of the country.

And to make the problem even more complex, Deere & Company is a global organization. So, this means that the company goes way beyond the local market. Obviously each one of these areas has varying requirements that are unique.

Mack observes that, "There are differences in the crops. There are differences in Deere & Company plant management conditions. There are differences in available resources in terms of suppliers. There are differences—strong differences—in cultures as you go from one country to another.

"The balancing act then is to try to fold as much commonness in as you can in order to control the total machine tool investment. But, at the same time, you have to be sensitive to the local requirements."

So, the many different New Generation models began to address these specific agricultural needs on an increasingly worldwide basis.

2010 1961–1965

The 2010 was more within the Waterloo New Generation family style with the same fenders, deluxe seat, and dash arrangement than was the smaller 1010.

This "family styling" was due largely to the fact that the research and development that began at Dubuque in 1955 was then moved to the Product Engineering Center at Waterloo in 1956.

Like the 1010, it used the "sleeve-and-deck" engine design. All 2010s were available with the Syncro-Range transmission giving eight forward and three reverse speeds. The four-cylinder engine was offered in gasoline, diesel, or LP gas versions.

The Special was an economy version of the Row-Crop Utility and available only with a diesel engine. It had a steel seat and smaller, shell fenders designed for export only. The 2010 was offered in these models:

Row-Crop Tractor (R)
Row-Crop Utility Tractor (RU)
Special Row-Crop Utility Tractor (RUS)
Hi-Crop Tractor (H)
Agricultural Crawler Tractor (CA)
Industrial Crawler (C)
Industrial Wheel Tractor (W)
Wheel Forklift (F)

This 2010 Hi-Crop looks showroom new, and is unique in that it has almost all of the important options. This includes power steering, universal three-point hitch, and front rockshaft. Thanks to 34 inches of clearance under the axles, the 2010 Hi-Crop could cultivate row crops later in the growing season without damage better than other tractors could.

Tachometer indicates just 695.4 hours have been recorded since new. Top speed in "road gear" or seventh gear was approximately 14 miles per hour, even though the spec sheet mentions "speeds to nearly 20 miles per hour." The gearshift on this early 2010 Row-Crop is on the console.

Built in 1965, this 2010 Row-Crop with narrow front Roll-O-Matic has only 695 hours on its tachometer. Virtually everything is still as original as when it departed the John Deere factory: paint, trim, tires, steering wheel, and seat. The engine provided up to 45 horsepower at the PTO.

The front rockshaft for a front-mounted cultivator has a chain leading to a three-point hitch attachment. Raising the three-point hitch also raised the front cultivator.

2010 Row-Crop Tractor

Able to handle a three-bottom plow or four-row cultivator, the 2010 had the flexibility to be the big tractor on a small acreage or a small tractor on a big acreage. It could get the job done quickly, comfortably, and economically. It could also handle a mounted corn picker or cotton picker.

It was available with gasoline, diesel, or LP gas engine; manual or power steering; regular or deluxe seat; conventional dual wheels, Roll-O-Matic dual wheels, wide adjustable front axle, or single front; front-mounted lights; fender-mounted lights; combination front- and fender-mounted lights; dual fender-mounted lights.

2010 Row-Crop Utility Tractor

This was the second most popular 2010 just behind the Row-Crop tractor. Its 20-inch clearance wasn't enough for tall row crops such as corn or cane, but it was well-suited for other, shorter row crops.

Like the others in the line, it was available with a choice of gasoline, diesel, or LP gas engine rated at 45 PTO horsepower.

2010 Hi-Crop Tractor

This Hi-Crop tractor was quite popular and was sold widely throughout the United States as well as overseas. "High, wide, and mighty handy for growers of tall, bushy or bedded crops" was the punchline on some of the Deere & Company advertisements.

It had the full power and full options of all of the 2010 tractors.

Rather than being an "experimental" tractor subjected to testing by John Deere engineers, this 2010 is instead an "experimenting" tractor. It's a dependable mainstay of the Department of Biological and Agricultural Engineering at the University of California, Davis. It's used by researchers who hang all sorts of strange gizmos on it. This particular arrangement shows a global positioning system antenna on the cab roof, with a one-of-a-kind experimental rig on the three-point hitch that measures the amount of compaction in the soil.

The 2020 High Utility tractor featured a two-stage clutch. Depress the pedal halfway, and the transmission disengaged. Push the clutch all the way down, and the PTO disengaged. This allowed the PTO to keep running while the tractor was stopped, which was helpful when working in especially heavy crops or trying to clear a developing clog-up.

Hit 'em where it means the most is the thought behind this back cover page from John Deere's *The Furrow* magazine. "John Deere New Generation tractors can put new earning power into any farm" certainly was a slogan that was sure to draw farmers' interest.

2010 Agricultural Crawler Tractor 1962–1965

The 2010 Agricultural Crawler wasn't a high-volume seller, as only 159 came off the production line. It was the last of Deere & Company's ag crawlers. *Tractor Digest*, published by *Two-Cylinder*, says it was believed to be was an Industrial Crawler painted green. Although a gasoline model was offered, none were produced.

It was available with either a constant-mesh four-speed manual shift or Hi-Lo-Reverse four-speed hydraulic shift transmission. Options included a double hydraulic system, universal three-point hitch, 1,000-rpm PTO assembly, front hitch, swinging drawbar, and full lighting equipment.

Both the Agricultural Crawler and Industrial Crawler were produced at the Dubuque facility.

Next
It's logical that the 2510 be considered a "10 Series" tractor. In this case, logic isn't correct. The 2510 was actually introduced after the first "20" tractors came out. The 2510 was the smallest New Generation Row-Crop. The 2510 was available with any of five front ends, gas or diesel engine, and either Synchro-Range or Power Shift.

The three-point hydraulic hitch and PTO are main features of the 2510 tractor.

2010 PRODUCTION

Prod. Year*	Row-Crop			Row-Crop Utility			Special Row-Crop Utility
	Gas	LP	Diesel	Gas	LP	Diesel	Diesel
1960	147	0	7	830	0	5	0
1961	3,447	119	1,685	2,625	44	1,416	0
1962	2,097	90	1,015	2,207	27	751	253
1963	2,032	87	780	2,443	41	692	739
1964	1,918	62	889	2,243	46	791	1,661
1965**	1,550	44	1,402	1,711	19	634	2,422
Total	11,191	402	5,778	12,059	177	4,289	5,075

Prod. Year*	Agricultural Hi-Crop			Industrial Crawler		Crawler	Crawler
	Gas	LP	Diesel	Gas	Diesel	Gas	Diesel
1960	2	0	0	0	0	0	0
1961	49	5	68	0	0	0	0
1962	32	1	68	0	0	301	1,202
1963	27	0	78	0	36	442	2,727
1964	11	1	77	0	97	387	4,018
1965**	12	0	57	0	26	6	246
Total	133	7	348	0	159	1,136	8,193

Prod. Year*	Industrial Wheel		Wheel Forklift	
	Gas	Diesel	Gas	Diesel
1960	7	0	0	0
1961	403	291	0	0
1962	478	451	0	0
1963	550	622	0	0
1964	597	972	117	19
1965**	555	1,207	162	19
Total	2,590	3,543	279	38

* Normal production years ran from November 1 through October 31, or the week ending nearest that date. Model years began following the midsummer annual inventory and maintenance shutdown. As a result, tractors built in 1960 are 1961 models, those built from August on in 1961 are 1962 models.
** Production of 2010 models ceased in September 1965.

Production code information wasn't included on the serial number plate. Serial number plates are located on the right side of the engine block.
These are the codes for each of the eight model types:
BA = Agricultural Crawler
BB = Industrial Crawler
BD = Row-Crop Utility
BE = Row-Crop
BF = Hi-Crop
BG = Industrial Wheel
BK = Special Row-Crop Utility
BN = Wheel Forklift

Even though this 2510 has been so completely restored inside and outside that it looks virtually showroom new, the recording tachometer confesses that it's seen almost 5,400 hours of field time.

2020 1965–1971

The 2020 benefited from the Deere & Company worldwide engineering effort. LP gas model sales were falling, so this model was sold only with four-cylinder diesel and gasoline engines. An LP gas model was no longer available.

As in the other models, the two-stage foot clutch allowed the PTO to continue running while the tractor's forward motion was stopped if the foot clutch was depressed halfway. The tractor was available with a foot-engaged differential lock that provided equal power to both rear wheels in slippery conditions.

The 2020 was offered in these models outfitted with the same range of standard, optional, and special equipment:

Low Utility Tractor (LU)
Row-Crop Utility Tractor (RU)
High Utility Tractor (HU)
Grove and Orchard Tractor (O)

2510 1966–1968

The smallest of New Generation tricycle row-crop tractors, the 2510 was still a true New Generation model. It featured all the goodies of the bigger Waterloo models such as Power Shift or Syncro-Range transmission. Engine options included a four-cylinder gasoline or diesel engine that tested out at 55 PTO horsepower. The models are:

Row-Crop Tractor (R)
Row-Crop Utility Tractor (RU)
Utility Tractor (U)
Hi-Crop Tractor (H)

An immaculate 1969, this 2520 is the first year of the series.

Rarer than rare, this is the only 2510 Hi-Crop gasoline Power Shift tractor John Deere ever made.

Front-end options were dual-wheel tricycle, regular or heavy-duty Roll-O-Matic, and a regular adjustable or a wide adjustable front axle. This made the 2510 a versatile tractor for almost any farming operation.

This is one of the few models that lists a "cigar lighter" instead of the usual cigarette lighter. Could this be a result of Harold Brock's influence?

Brock was a cigar man, at least in his youth. The story is told about the day while he was employed at Ford Motor Company, working as an engineer in the tractor division. He was doing some field testing when Henry Ford came to the field and asked Brock what he was doing with his cigar. Ford was very much against smoking.

Brock replied that the mosquitoes were so bad that he thought he had to do something to attempt to repel them. The next day Ford had the field sprayed for mosquitoes.

2520 1969–1973

The 2520's 61 PTO horsepower was up more than 10 percent from that of the 2510's 55 PTO horsepower.

This was due to refinements in piston and ring design, plus cylinder block and liner improvements. Another important option that was available for the 2520 was the Roll-Gard cab. The 2520 was offered in these models:

Row-Crop Tractor (R)
Utility Tractor (U)
Hi-Crop Tractor (H)

Waiting to be restored, this 2520 Hi-Crop gas Synchro-Range transmission tractor had worked for almost three decades. The main difference between a 2510 and 2520 is an additional 6 horsepower, hence a new designation.

What made the 2010 Row-Crop tractor tick is fully described in this descriptive sheet. Note that the four front end assembly options are considered so important that they're illustrated.

Front view of 2510 shows wide-spaced wheels on a wide adjustable front axle.

6

THE 3000 AND 4000 SERIES

3010 1961–1963

Talk to almost any retired Deere & Company engineer who worked in Waterloo during the preparation and launch of the New Generation tractors, and he'll quickly point out that he considers the 3010 and 4010 to be the only "real" New Generation tractors.

His rationale? Yes, the 1010 and 2010 bear a strong family resemblance with the other New Generation models. But only the 3010 and 4010 actually initially incorporated the features that identified the New Generation tractors.

The 3010 was a Waterloo product with a 55-horsepower four-cylinder engine available in gasoline, diesel, or LP gas. It featured closed-center hydraulics that provided up to three independent "live" hydraulic circuits. Also standard were power steering, power brakes, and power rockshaft. The Syncro-Range transmission provided eight forward and three reverse speeds.

The 3010 and 4010 were tractors that fulfilled the expectations of both Deere & Company and farmers. It's one "bug" concerning a water-pump problem was both unexpected and troublesome.

Warren Wiele, retired Deere & Company engineer, remembers the water pump problem: "We'd not made castings of that nature before. We were making engines of the type we'd never built before, and so we probably didn't know everything we needed to know about getting those castings clean. When some of that sand got in there, it would chew up that water-pump seal rather quickly."

Engineers and service personnel had some not-so-pleasant, memories of this problem before it was solved. The 3010 was offered in these models:

Row-Crop Tractor (R)
Standard Tractor
Row-Crop Utility Tractor (RU)
Grove and Orchard Tractor (O)

3020 1964–1972

With 65 PTO horsepower compared to the 3010's 60 PTO horsepower, the 3020 moved up slightly in the horsepower race. Equipped with the Power Shift transmission, it allowed shifting between eight forward or four reverse speeds without clutching. The Syncro-Range transmission was still available. A hydrostatic power front-wheel drive was added in 1968 to the list of available options.

The 3020 was offered in these models:

Row-Crop Tractor (R)
Row-Crop Utility Tractor (RU)
Standard Tractor
Hi-Crop Tractor (H)
Orchard and Grove Tractor (O)

This tractor might look like an immaculately restored 3010 Row-Crop Diesel, but it's also much more: On its rear end, it carries serial number 1000. According to John Deere's numbering system, this means this was the first 3010 to be rolled down the assembly line at the Waterloo, Iowa, manufacturing plant. Buyers of the 55-PTO-horsepower tractors could customize them with conventional dual front wheels, regular or heavy-duty single front wheel, regular or heavy-duty Roll-O-Matic "knee-action" duals, or adjustable front axle.

3010 PRODUCTION

Row-Crop				Standard		
Prod. Year	*Gas*	*LP*	*Diesel*	*Gas*	*LP*	*Diesel*
1960	160	67	3,391	3	0	307
1961	5,483	976	7,971	302	45	1,113
1962	3,507	734	6,450	84	36	826
1963**	3,375	665	5,863	104	22	771
Total	12,525	2,442	23,675	493	103	3,017

Special Row-Row-Crop Utility				Orchard		Crop Utility
*Prod. Year**	*Gas*	*LP*	*Diesel*	*Gas*	*Diesel*	*Diesel*
1960	4	0	9	0	0	0
1961	405	24	722	0	0	0
1962	120	3	185	12	36	82
1963**	125	5	192	7	21	36
Total	654	32	1,108	19	57	118

Industrial			Lanz Special Standard
Prod. Year	*Gas*	*Diesel*	*Diesel*
1960	4	0	0
1961	118	283	0
1962	37	208	0
1963**	33	157	139
Total	192	648	139

* Normal production years ran from November 1 through October 31, or the week ending nearest that date. Model years began following the midsummer annual inventory and maintenance shutdown. So tractors built in 1960 are 1961 models; those built from August on in 1961 are 1962 models.

** Production of 3010 models ceased July 1963.

Production Codes (Serial Number Prefix):

First digit = 1 (Indicates 3000 Series)
Second digit = Model type

Second digit codes:
1 = Row Crop
2 = Standard
4 = Row-Crop Utility
5 = Industrial
6 = Special Row-Crop Utility
7 = Lanz Special Standard
8 = Orchard
Number 3 wasn't used, as it was reserved for Hi-Crop Tractors.

Note: A third digit in the serial number prefix indicated fuel type. This prefix was recorded in factory serial number records, but wasn't stamped into the serial number plate until midsummer 1963, starting with 1964 3020 production.

Examples of serial numbers as shown on serial number plates:

11 T 1060	Row-Crop
12 T 6868	Standard
14 T 4762	Row-Crop Utility
15 T 10622	Industrial
18 T 28413	Orchard

Note that variations in the format shown above are possible; however, the examples provide the typical coding and serial number layout.

There weren't too many 3010 LP tractors made. This 3010 LP is still working in the fields after more than three decades of service. It was the only model that carried the LP tank where the gasoline tank was usually located in gas tractors.

Serial number 1000 verifies that this is the first 3010 to be produced.

Although about to be restored and not at the peak of its beauty, this 1961 3010 Row-Crop Utility LP was one of only 32 ever manufactured by John Deere.

That's an LP tank, not a gasoline tank. Only in this particular model 3010 LP was the LP tank situated where the gasoline tank normally was positioned.

The 4000 Series
4010 1961–1963

The 4010 aptly demonstrated the high-horsepower-to-weight design of the new Deere line. For example, the older Model 730 weighed 6,790 pounds and was rated at 53.66 drawbar horsepower. In contrast, the 4010 weighed in at 6,980 pounds but generated 73.65 drawbar horsepower. This represented a 37 percent increase in drawbar horsepower, yet only a 3 percent increase in tractor weight.

The 4010 line used a six-cylinder for all engines, gasoline, diesel, or LP gas, plus a Syncro-Range transmission. The 4010 was one of the most copied designs in tractor history.

The 4010 was offered in these models:

Standard Tractor
Row-Crop Tractor (R)
Row-Crop Utility Tractor (RU)
Hi-Crop Tractor (H)

4010 Production

Prod. Year*	Special Row-Crop			Standard			Standard
	Gas	LP	Diesel	Gas	LP	Diesel	Diesel
1960	57	68	3,807	3	0	62	0
1961	1,573	1,120	11,084	46	315	3,995	0
1962	837	1,575	10,768	20	297	3,579	34
1963**	1,146	1,696	11,077	29	180	3,134	1
Total	3,613	4,459	36,736	98	792	11,370	35

Prod. Year*	Hi-Crop			Industrial	
	Gas	LP	Diesel	Gas	Diesel
1960	0	0	0	0	4
1961	0	7	48	1	32
1962	1***	8	60	5	181
1963**	0	2	62	4	55
Total	1***	17	170	10	272

* Normal production years ran from November 1 through October 31, or the week ending nearest that date. Model years began following the midsummer annual inventory and maintenance shutdown. Tractors built in 1960 are 1961 models; those built from August to December 1961 are 1962 models.

** Production of 4010 models ceased in July 1963.

*** The only 4010 gas Hi-Crop built was recalled, rebuilt into a Diesel Hi-Crop, and its serial number renumbered.

Production Codes (Serial Number Prefix):

First digit = 2 (Indicates 4000 Series)
Second digit = Model type

Second digit codes:
1 = Row-Crop
2 = Standard
3 = Hi-Crop
5 = Industrial
6 = Special Standard

Note: A third digit in the serial number prefix indicated fuel type. This prefix was recorded in factory serial number records but wasn't stamped into the serial number plate until midsummer, 1963, starting with 1964 4020 production.

Examples of serial numbers as shown on serial number plates:

21 T 1355	Row-Crop
22 T 1317	Standard
23 T 9045	Hi-Crop
25 T 1554	Industrial
26 T35996	Special Standard

Note: Variations in the format shown above are possible; however, the examples provide the typical coding and serial number layout.

Just three years after the 3010 was introduced, its replacement, the 3020, was on the way. A more powerful tractor, the 3020 also excelled in having the Power Shift transmission. This enabled the driver with a single lever to shift into any of eight forward speeds, or four reverse, without clutching, even on the go under load.

This is the instrument panel of a rare 3010 Row-Crop Utility LP. Only 32 were made. Note both the LP knobs and the "crooked" gearshift lever.

4020 1964–1972

Two years into 4020 production, the Roll-Gard was perfected by Deere & Company engineers. Roll-Gard is a Deere & Company trademark name for the rollover protective structure (ROPS) the company pioneered. It was first offered in 1966 on the 4020 and other New Generation tractors.

Retired Deere & Company engineer Warren Wiele provided insight into this safety project. He noted that one of the reasons the ocean liner Titanic sank was because the steel in the ship had what's called "cold tem-perature embrittlement." He said early versions of the Deere ROPS suffered from the same problem—little defects in the steel that aren't a problem until the temperature is much lower than normal. Wiele explains:

I have a video of experimental John Deere tractors being run up a hill and tipped over backward to test their Roll-Gards. The video illustrates what happened when the roll guard was packed in dry ice (to simulate cold temperatures). The roll bar, in this case, didn't even slow down the 4020 tractor.

This 3020 left the factory with a gas engine and Power Shift transmission; however, the engine used too much gas and was relatively low in horsepower for its weight. So after the building of an adapter plate, the engine was replaced with a John Deere industrial tractor diesel "Dubuque" engine. Fuel efficiency improved considerably, and available horsepower jumped from 70 to 105—a 50 percent boost. Bottom line: This modified 3020 delivers virtually the same horsepower as a late 4020 tractor.

In normal temperatures it would have done the job quite well; however, when the steel's temperature was reduced, the roll bar would fail due to the effects of this cold temperature embrittlement.

Of course, the farmer isn't going to stay out of his tractor just because it's cold outside. So we finally had to go to a special steel to avoid the problem.

The video Wiele mentioned not only shows the tractor falling over backward and the steering wheel burying itself into the chest of a mannequin driver, it also shows a Deere engineer, standing off to the side, who throws his hands up in the air, takes off his hat, and slams it down onto the ground.

Wiele also explained how the rollover was created. He described how someone would stand behind the tractor with a long rope hooked up to the clutch pedal. With the engine revved, the tractor would be sent up this really steep embankment. Just before it got to the top, the rope would be pulled so that the clutch could be popped. It would give the tractor enough momentum to go over backward.

"I certainly was glad that I wasn't the man behind the tractor with the rope," Wiele said. "Later on, we developed much more sophisticated methods of testing."

Another feature that began as an exclusive on the 4020 was power front-wheel drive.

Originally offered in gasoline, diesel, or LP gas, the LP gas 4020 model was later dropped.

In 1968, these tractors were available with an optional hydrostatic power front-wheel drive. A hydraulic power differential lock was introduced on the 4020. This allowed the operator to depress a foot pedal to improve traction. The deferential lock directed power to both back wheels equally to provide better pulling power in situations where the rear wheels began to slip.

The 4020 was offered in these models:

Standard Tractor
Row-Crop Tractor (R)
Row-Crop Utility Tractor (RU)
Hi-Crop Tractor (H)

4320 1971–1972

The 4320 was dubbed the "super 4020" due to its turbocharger that boosted power to 115 PTO horsepower from a six-cylinder diesel engine.

New 20.8x34 tires were engineered to capture all the added power of the 4320 too. Other than a weight increase of approximately 700 pounds, the 4320 was pretty much just a hopped-up 4020 with most of its same standard equipment and options including Power Front-Wheel-Drive.

4510 1968

The 4510 was an experimental unit that didn't actually see production or sales according to engineers who worked on the project. It did, however, serve as a testing ground for a turbocharged engine design that was perfected and later introduced as the 4520.

It inspired, with a little help from designer Dreyfuss, one interesting style change and a couple of interesting stories.

Dreyfuss didn't like the exhaust and air cleaner stacks that "polluted" the clean lines of the tractor hood. He was constantly asking if they could be eliminated. The engineers accommodated him by designing the air-cleaner intake and filter to fit under the hood. Service access was permitted via a hinged door at the rear of the hood near the cowling.

Dreyfuss was so pleased with this change that he told the engineers he was going to send them a check for a case of Scotch whiskey. And he did send the check

Built in the United States but sold first to a Canadian farmer in a prairie province, this 3020 Wheatland model differed from the other 3020s in several ways. It moved on a narrower front end, had larger fenders, was designed for pulling and so didn't mount a three-point hitch, and the driver mounted from the rear rather than from the side.

Expect no agreement of aficionados of New Generation tractors concerning which was the most important in the 10 Series. However, few can argue that the 4010 doesn't combine everyday brawn with balanced elegance even better than its stablemates. This 4010 Row-Crop was the very first 4010 to be manufactured. The 4010 series delivered 80 PTO horsepower. The 4010 personified the "new generation of power" with its high horsepower-to-weight ratio.

to Deere & Company's engineering department, along with the promise of another case of Scotch if the engineers would also get rid of the exhaust stack. The check, however, was returned accompanied by a thank-you note.

4520 1969–1970

This was the first Deere & Company tractor to be sold with a factory-installed turbocharger. It also featured a bigger lubricating system, larger radiator and fan, bigger capacity air cleaner, and redesigned block for more coolant flow.

Retired Deere & Company engineer Danny Gleeson says the tractor didn't use another model frame, but instead used an entirely new frame designed for only the 4520. The entire tractor was made bigger and better in an effort to supply more power to horsepower-hungry customers.

This tractor also inspired Dreyfuss, but in a different fashion. Gleeson recalls the incident this way:

"We moved into the new PEC center in 1956. It was probably some time in 1957 or early 1958 when Dreyfuss saw one of the experimental tractors in actual hardware form. He'd been looking at models most of the time before this. Then he got up on this tractor and looked at it.

"What we call the cowl, the sheet metal covering over the instrument panel where it met the hood, gave us a deuce of a time getting it worked out. We finally said we'll just have to fasten it with cap screws. So we used four cap screws to hold this cowl on, two on each side.

"When Henry saw that, he just immediately read me the riot act, up one side and down the other. He likened me to an engineer who might work for General Motors on a Cadillac automobile, and when the car was finished, put four cap screws right in the middle of the hood.

"He never did forgive me for that, although it went into production with those four cap screws."

This late 1972 4020 Diesel has only 1,767 hours on its tachometer, quite low for more than a quarter of a century of life after leaving the Waterloo, Iowa, plant. Belying the tractor's age, the original paint shines like new.

4620 1971–1972

Air and fuel in the right mixture is essential for proper combustion within the cylinder. More fuel without more air is a waste of fuel with no increase in horsepower. A turbocharger forces compressed air into the combustion chamber and so allows more fuel to be used. This correct mixture of more air and more fuel results in increased horsepower.

When the art of turbocharging reached a plateau, engineers responded by cooling the air, which was then heated in the compression process. The more dense cooled air produced better fuel and air combustion. An intercooler was the resulting innovation.

With this new feature, the 4620's six-cylinder diesel engine churned out 135 PTO horsepower.

4000 1969–1972

Using the same engine as the 4020, but weighing in at 7,670 pounds as compared to 8,555 pounds for the 4020, the concept behind the 4000 was the pushing of the limits of the high horsepower-to-weight ratio. Pulling smaller implements faster to accomplish the same amount of work was the underlying principle. Some people considered the 4000 to be similar to a 4010 with a 4020 engine.

The Syncro-Range transmission was standard, but the Power Shift could be ordered as an option. The 4000 was also available with Roll-Gard and a canopy for the Roll-Gard.

This 1962 4010 Diesel Row-Crop has a narrow front end so that with a mounted cornpicker, it could go down between the rows without knocking down any corn. This tractor was built only with Synchro Range transmission. A 4010 could have either a narrow front end or a wide front end and still be considered a Row-Crop tractor. Both the rear and front wheels can be adjusted for width on the Row-Crop.

One of the last 4020s manufactured, this 4020 Diesel developed 96 PTO horsepower in Nebraska tests. The last four years the 4020 was made, 1969 to 1972, the tractor was made with a right-side console for the hydraulic levers. The 1971–1972 models had a steering wheel that had more of a dished center. This brought the steering wheel a little bit closer to the driver. Earlier model steering wheels were flat. The last 4020 also had a longer, offset gearshift lever and an oval muffler for improved visibility.

This is the first 4010 Diesel sold by the Keystone, Iowa, John Deere dealer in 1960. The 4010 Diesel model has 85 horsepower, which is five more than the gas version.

This is the side console for the hydraulic levers on a late 1972 4020. The side console certainly made operating the hydraulics much handier in the 1969 to 1972 models. Why hasn't the original protective plastic been removed from the seat? The tractor's owner says that while leaving it on might detract slightly from its appearance, the tractor is worth more money in this condition.

Without a doubt, this rare 1966 4020 LP narrow front tractor is easily the most unusual-looking New Generation tractor to ever leave the factory. The large up-front, vision-obscuring tank detracted from its otherwise graceful, yet purposeful design. This particular tractor with three-point hitch mounts large rear tires.

When new in 1965, this 4020 Diesel High-Crop sold for $11,370. It and similar tractors were designed for cultivating sugar cane in the South and truck crops in California. It has 96 horsepower.

This 4020 Diesel carries serial number 65001, and it's the first Power Shift tractor manufactured by John Deere in 1964 when the 4020 replaced the 4010. The tractor has only 3,000 hours.

The 4000 gasoline-powered tractor at 94 horsepower has two fewer horsepower than the diesel model, and also considerably less torque. Only 256 4000 gas tractors with Synchro Range transmissions and roll guard canopies were ever produced by John Deere. The 4000 was an attempt by John Deere to fill a gap in its line-up of tractors in order to better compete against the International 706 tractor.

This particular 4000 Diesel is unusual because few exactly like it were made. Although the 4000 was a tractor designed for the economy-minded, this one uses the more expensive Power Shift transmission option. It has only 2,347 hours on its tachometer, and its paint is the original. The tractor came with absolutely no frills, such as battery covers or sheet metal around the seat to cover the hydraulics.

When this 4020 Diesel left the Waterloo, Iowa, plant in 1965, it was "loaded" with options. These included dual hydraulics, Power Shift, and wide front end.

Right
The Power Shift was a welcome addition to the right side of this 1965 4020 Diesel's instrument panel.

Only 46 4000 Low Profile tractors were ever built, and only 21 with the same Synchro Range transmission as used in this one. The 4000 Low Profile was targeted at grove and orchard operators who needed a combination of high horsepower and a low profile for clearance. Height was reduced throughout the tractor. It also has a shorter turning radius than other 4000 Series tractors. Due to demand by vineyard and orchard growers, the Fresno, California, John Deere dealer developed a low-profile modification. Company engineers liked the idea when they saw the tractor, and the 4000 Low Profile was the result. Approximately half were sold out to Fresno-area farmers.

Kind of a hybrid, too, the 4320 was basically a 4020 chassis. The exception was some gears in the transmission that were heavier. The synchronizers in reverse gear were eliminated, which allowed some gears to be made a little wider and stronger. The 4320 also had a wider hood to accommodate a bigger fuel tank and larger radiator. Although both the 4020 and 4320 shared the same 404-cubic inch engine, the 4320's engine was turbocharged to provide 116 PTO horsepower, according to Nebraska tests.

Just off the assembly line, this 4620 Diesel, the 459th made, was delivered to the John Deere Engineering Department and not to a dealership. Unique for its day, it had front-wheel assist, three selective control valves (SCVs), optional lighting, quick hitch, and a factory installed cab. The engine delivered a whopping 135 horsepower.

"3010" SERIES STANDARD TRACTORS

WATERLOO

New John Deere "3010" Standard Tractors provide the practical answer to the power requirements of medium- and large-acreage grain and rice growers. Their brand-new John Deere-built, variable-speed 4-cylinder gasoline, Diesel, and LP-Gas engines provide up to 55 horsepower at the PTO. The "3010" Standards are ruggedly built to turn out consistently good work, year after year with a minimum of costly down time.

The "3010" Standard has ample power to handle efficiently such large-capacity equipment as 4-bottom drawn and integral plows, 11-foot disk harrows, 12-foot disk tillers, 12-foot tool carriers, 20x7 grain drills and similar loads.

QUALITY FEATURES

A Short, Compact Design

Maximum field maneuverability is offered by this compactly built tractor permitting operators to dodge obstructions and make extremely short turns.

Wide Rear Fenders

Protection from dust, dirt and mud from rear wheels, and added safety on hillsides are offered by the wide rear fenders regularly furnished on these standard tractors.

Oscillating Front Axle

A generous 15-degree range of oscillation is provided in the front axle, making this tractor ideal for use in bedded land, checks, levees and other rough field conditions.

New Independent PTO

Both 540 and 1000 rpm equipment is handled with ease by the new Independent PTO . . . the most advanced PTO in tractor history.

New Variable-Speed Engines

The new, ruggedly built John Deere variable-speed gasoline, Diesel and LP-Gas engines offer fully governed power at any throttle setting . . . more flexible, responsive power matched to the job at hand.

New Syncro-Range Transmission

Greater shifting ease is provided by the new Syncro-Range Transmission that delivers an exact speed and power for every job . . . speeds ranging from a crawl to 20 mph.

New Hydraulic System

A unique demand-type pump and a tremendous reservoir capacity are features of the revolutionary hydraulic system that supplies an abundance of power to operate up to three independent circuits, plus new power steering and exclusive new power brakes.

New Universal 3-Point Hitch

All types of 3-point hitch equipment are easily handled by the new Universal 3-Point Hitch that provides Load Control, Depth Control or Load-and-Depth Control to match exact soil and job conditions. A new Quik-Coupler attachment lets operator attach and detach tools without leaving the tractor seat.

10-15-1

The spec sheet lists the many features and advantages provided by the 3010 Standard tractor. It points out that this tractor is the practical answer to the power needs of the medium to large grain or rice farm.

The 4320 Diesel was delivered with an entirely new tire size, 20.8-34. That's because John Deere engineers thought no existing tire size complemented the 4320 well enough. It also has increased cooling and oil capacities over the similar size 4020 engine.

THE 5000, 6000, 7000, 8000, & WORLDWIDE TRACTORS

5010 1963–1965

The 5010 was the first addition to the New Generation line of tractors. Powered by a six-cylinder diesel engine, it was factory observed at 117 PTO horsepower and 100 PTO at the drawbar.

It introduced Category 3 linkage in order to use equipment matched to its high horsepower. It was the first John Deere tractor with 1,000-rpm–only PTO.

The 5010 was the first two-wheel-drive tractor with more than 100 horsepower at both drawbar and PTO. It was aimed at the wheat-producing Great Plains where farms were growing larger and needed to work big acreage fast. The 5010 operator enjoyed the comforts of a deluxe seat, power brakes, power steering, wide rear fenders, and a dust shield.

It came equipped with a Syncro-Range transmission. Factory-installed, although not factory-built, cabs were an option. The cab offered a heater, but no air conditioning.

A new tire size was developed for the 4010 and could be ordered as an option. Also available was a dual wheel package.

5020 1966–1972

Carrying on the tradition established by the 5010, the 5020 was the first two-wheel-drive tractor with more than 130 horsepower. In 1967, a row-crop version was introduced that was the most powerful row-crop tractor available on the market at the time. The features and options of the 5020 were consistent with those of the 5010.

Models included:

Standard Tractor
Row-Crop Utility Tractor (RU)

The 6000 Tractors
6030 1972–1977

One of the last additions to the New Generation line was the 6030. It carried the 30 Series designation and was available well into the 1970s. It was equipped with an impressive six-cylinder, 531-cubic inch, valve-in-head, variable-speed, turbocharged, and intercooled diesel engine. And it featured the same 175 PTO horsepower engine that was developed for the 7520 tractor.

The 6030 was essentially the 5020 with a newly designed engine. It was the first Deere & Company tractor to offer a choice of engines: either the naturally aspirated version or the turbocharged and intercooled model.

Factory-installed cabs, but not Deere built, could also be ordered for the Standard Tractor and Row-Crop Utility Tractor (RU).

7020 1971–1975

This wasn't the first Deere four-wheel-drive tractor, although some people think it was. It was preceded by the 8010 in 1959. The 7020's 145 PTO horsepower six-cylinder diesel engine was considered a bit underpowered by some users. The Syncro-Range transmission was standard equip-

Farmers really liked the four-wheel-drive 7020, with one exception: lack of enough horsepower. The 7520 was developed to respond to that need. Its 531-cubic-inch engine at 175 PTO horsepower provided an additional 25 horsepower over that of the 7020.

There never was a 6010 or a 6020 tractor. And, when the 6030 came out in 1972, it predated the 30 series of tractors that didn't arrive until a year later. This 1972 model put out a strong 175 horsepower at the PTO. It was powered by a new six-cylinder valve-in-head, variable-speed, turbocharged, intercooled "Turbo-Built" engine. It came with either duals or single wheels and in Row-Crop or Standard models.

5010 PRODUCTION

700	Standard	Industrial (Offset)	JD
Prod.			
Year			
1962	1,042	0	0
1963	1,778	557	0
1964	1,409	794	0
1965	1,234	656	83
Total	5,463	2,007	83

Production Codes Number Plates (Serial Number Prefix):
First digit = 3 (Indicates 5000 Series)
Second digit = Model type
Third digit = Fuel type

Second digit codes:
2 = Standard
5 = JD700
7 = Industrial (Offset)

Third digit code:
3 = Diesel

Note: Fuel codes weren't used until the 1964 model year.

Examples of serial numbers as shown on serial number plates:
1962–1963 models:
32 T 1234   Standard
37 T 2896   Industrial (Offset)
1964–1965 models:
SNT323R010678R   Standard
SNT353R010630R   JD700
SNT373R010060R   Industrial (Offset)

ment that could be coupled with an optional Hi-Lo feature to increase the standard eight forward speeds to 16. Other features included power steering, plus power brakes on the rear-wheels. It had a closed-center hydraulic system with two remote-cylinder outlets. A transmission-driven 1,000-rpm PTO was optional.

A Roll-Gard cab was standard with the option of either or both heater and air conditioning. This cab wasn't manufactured by Deere & Company but was instead an after-market unit that fit around Deere's ROTS.

Either Category 2 or 3 implements could be mounted with its Quick-Coupler Hitch.

The 7020 featured dual-wheel ability on all four wheels, with a wide range of wheel width adjustments. By selecting a narrow tire and wheel option, the tractor could be used for row-crop cultivation. This was an entirely new concept for four-wheel-drive tractors. Even though it was a "big" machine, the narrow hood provided good visibility for row-crop work.

When Harold Brock first joined the engineering department at Deere, he was an assistant in the research area. He remembered a company named Wagner that was selling four-wheel-drive, articulated tractors in a few states out West and in the Wheat Belt.

"The idea was to design a wheeled tractor to replace the big Caterpillar crawlers," Brock said. "Deere & Company supplied implements for Caterpillar crawlers for years, so we finally built some four-wheel-drive tractors, mostly for testing. This tractor was called the 8010.

"We bought all of the components for the unit, because we didn't want to tool up for the limited sales volume that was estimated. I think we probably bought from the same major suppliers that Wagner used."

Brock remembered the tractor was very expensive. "It had to retail something

When this 5010 wheeled into its first field in 1963, it was the largest row-crop tractor built anywhere in the world at the time. It had 116 PTO horsepower under its long hood. Actually, most of the 5010s made by John Deere were painted industrial yellow and used outside of agriculture. Then a few large row-crop farmers started using them for pulling the bigger equipment coming into vogue—and the trend to larger and larger tractors was on its way.

The 5010 tractor described in this sheet is called the "most powerful standard tractor on the market." It provided a hefty 100 horsepower at the drawbar and 117 horsepower at the PTO.

5010 TRACTOR
WATERLOO

It's the most-powerful standard tractor on the market—the new John Deere "5010." This New Generation Tractor, powered by a 6-cylinder variable-speed Diesel engine, develops 117 h.p. measured at the PTO . . . more than 100 h.p. at the drawbar. It is ideally suited for large-acreage grain and rice growers, for any farmer with heavy tillage require-ments. Just look at the "following" this "5010" has: up to 40 feet of grain drill, 32-foot disk tillers, 27-foot disk harrow, 7-bottom semi-integral plow, 42 feet of rod weeder, 34 feet of field cultivator, 32 feet of mulch treader, a 22-foot tool carrier, and similar loads. This tractor pays its own way in terms of in-creased work output and lower per-acre costs.

The "5010" is not a "warmed-over" tractor. It's brand new from front grille to drawbar and fully capable of producing and efficiently using 117 horsepower.

QUALITY FEATURES

Tremendous Capacity

The "5010" handles large equipment at maximum working speeds, enabling one man to accomplish more work in any given time. Full advantage can be taken of every break in the weather, the requirement for additional drivers is reduced, acreage expansion is encouraged, and the limitations of equipment size have been rolled back. Never before has there been a tractor with such carrying power for wide-horizon farming.

Variable-Speed Engine

A brand-new, John Deere-designed-and-built, 6-cyl-inder variable-speed engine permits using any part or all of the 117 horsepower that the job demands. It's a heavy-duty engine with large, heavy parts such as a 7-main-bearing crankshaft providing ample power to lug through tough spots.

Large Tires

A tire of entirely new size—24.5 x 32—was developed for the "5010." This tire places two feet of tread-width per tire on the ground, improving traction and flotation. Weight-carrying capacity of the tire is also greatly in-creased. Both regular bar-type and deep-lugged cane and rice type are available. Front tires also are larger (11.00 x 16) for greater front-end flotation.

Syncro-Range Transmission

A new Syncro-Range Transmission, with ample strength to utilize the higher horsepower of the "5010," provides eight overlapping gear selections. Ground travel speed and power can be pinpointed to each job for better-quality work. Constant-mesh gear design, on-the-go shifting within each of the four ranges, and di-rection-reverser action are other features of this fine transmission that make good work fast—easy.

Independent Power Take-Off

Big-capacity power-driven equipment can be handled with maximum efficiency—thanks to the new 1000 rpm independent PTO. A 1-1/2 mph "creeper" gear, plus the ability to stop tractor travel without affecting PTO operation, lets the operator handle heavy crops with ease and efficiency . . . practically eliminates clogging.

Power Steering and Brakes

Power steering and power brakes (both regular equip-ment) make the "5010" as easy to drive and maneuver as a much smaller tractor. Light pressure on the steering wheel puts tremendous hydraulic power to work to turn the front wheels in deep sand, mud, and snow. Power brakes make possible extremely short turns at the ends of the field and positively stop heavy loads.

This 5020 now carries a 5050 decal because it's half John Deere and half Cummins. It was much more difficult to adapt the longer, bulkier Cummins 855 Diesel than it was the somewhat smaller Detroit Diesel V-8. This engine churns out 400 horsepower and a hunk of torque.

on the order of $30,000. This was at a time when the largest tractor we had, the 5010, sold for only $10,000. So it wasn't a really cost-effective project."

Deere decided to scrap the four-wheel-drive idea after this project was judged to be prohibitively expensive. The company would re-enter this business years later with the model 7020, a unit made from existing ag tractor components rather than purchased components.

"What we did with the 7020 was to take the 4020 and bisect it and put an engine in the middle," Brock remembered. "By doing so we took advantage of high-volume production components. This brought the price down.

"We took our high production parts and put them together and found that we could sell our tractor for $13,000. That put us in the four-wheel-drive business. The 7020 was also good, because its components could all be serviced by the dealer, same as with our ag component tractors."

7520 1972–1975

Almost identical in style, appearance, and features as the 7020, the 7520 was equipped with the impressive 175 PTO-horsepower, six-cylinder "turbo-built" diesel engine also featured in the 6030 tractor.

The extra horsepower helped meet the growing "power addiction" of large agricultural operations.

The 8000 Tractors
8010/8020 1959

The 8010 was introduced in 1959 at Marshalltown, Iowa. The event was a John Deere field day at which new products were introduced to distributors and dealers. Was this tractor really a decoy to divert any suspicion that Deere & Company was going to discontinue its long-lived two-cylinder?

Hewitt said there wasn't a conscious effort to do so. On the other hand, Fred Hileman, retired Waterloo service director, believes that it was. In any event, the 8010 was a harbinger of the many good things to come in the next decade.

The 8010 was a tractor designed around parts that Deere & Company purchased from other manufacturers. The low number of sales anticipated didn't warrant the cost of tooling required for the company to produce its own components in-house.

In all truth, the 8010 was far advanced for its time and offered features that wouldn't be found on other tractors for years, if ever. Its grease bank was a notable example. Everything that needed lubrication on the tractor, except for the universal joints and a couple of hinges, could be greased from this single, easily accessible location. Open the door of the battery compartment and there was a lubrication chart on the inside of the door for quick reference, similar to that of today's combines.

It also featured two different hydraulic systems, front wheels that could be shifted in and out to eliminate excessive tire wear on the road, air brakes, and a hydraulic clutch. And the air system could be used to inflate the tractor's own tires. Its red taillights were set into the fenders, just as they are on today's new tractors.

Also, when the headlights were on, there was a courtesy light at both sets of steps and another light in the toolbox area. Roughly half of the 8010s were delivered with Category 5 three-point hitches.

The records aren't definite, but the indication is that 100 or perhaps a few more 8010s were manufactured before the program was halted. Only two were ever sold east of the Mississippi River. Actually, Deere & Company had some difficulty selling its 8010s at all.

Farmers would flock to fields to see a monster 8010 throwing dirt from the multitude of moldboards it pulled, but they were hesitant to buy. The company eventually resorted to renting out many of its 8010s before selling them. Several were returned to the Waterloo plant to serve for years as powerful yard tractors.

Within several years, all but one 8010 was recalled and rebuilt at the factory with a heavier duty transmission and clutch. All these 8010s were then renumbered and returned with decals showing they were now 8020 models.

The 8020 weighed in at an impressive 26,350 pounds with liquid ballast in the tires, and measured just 2 inches short of 20 feet. Its engine was a GM 671E two-cycle six-cylinder diesel rated at 206 engine and 150 drawbar horsepower.

Worldwide New Generation Tractors

After the worldwide tractor program was in place, Europe and Argentina Deere & Company factories began producing their versions of the New Generation tractors.

820 1968–1973

The 820 was the smallest in the New Generation tractor line. Manufactured both in the United States and at the Deere Mannheim Works in Mannheim, Germany, it was powered by a three-cylinder, 31 PTO horsepower diesel engine.

The 820 is unusual, because two different Deere & Company tractors carried the 820 designation. The two-cylinder 820 diesel was produced at Waterloo, Iowa, from 1956 to 1958.

A decade later, the 820 three-cylinder was manufactured at both Waterloo and Mannheim.

While the 820 was small, it had many of the bigger tractor features, including collar shift transmission with eight forward and four reverse gears, rockshaft, and Category 1 three-point hitch. The deluxe seat and power steering was offered as an option.

1120

This was Mannheim's version of the 1520. Much of the production was shipped to the Canadian market.

2120

This was another Mannheim tractor that was specifically produced for the Canadian market.

The original 5010 and 5020 tractors were relatively underpowered at 133 horsepower from a 531 cubic inch six cylinder engine, and cumbersome due to their weight. A late model 4020 with its 100 horsepower and lighter weight could keep right with a 5020. Thanks to the 5010's and 5020's well-built transmissions and rear ends, either Row-Crop or Wheatland models were converted to Detroit Diesel 8V71 V-8 engines developing 275 to 318 horsepower, depending on which injectors were used. Approximately 100 such conversions were produced between 1968 and 1974.

New Generation Tractors on Steroids

The compulsion to make everything bigger and more powerful is half human nature and half necessity. The human nature aspect is perhaps wired somewhere deep in the psyche of the human male, just awaiting the fitting moment to manifest itself. This "moment" is usually linked to the correlation that bigger and more powerful is always perceived as better.

The "necessity" half of the equation resonates with the "better mouse trap" theory. This compulsive behavior, once focused on John Deere tractors, brought moment and necessity together, resulting in some remarkable versions of the New Generation tractors.

The 5010 was Deere's first tractor to breech the century mark in both PTO and drawbar horsepower. During the years from the first 1963 model through 1965, it was a good big-acreage tractor. The succeeding 5020 increased power to 140 PTO horsepower.

During this same period the 4010 was upgraded to the 4020, making the late model 4020 diesel just shy of 97 PTO horsepower. And, because of its lighter weight, it could perform side-by-side with the 5010, and in some conditions also with the 5020.

On the flip side, the 5010 and 5020 had superior weight, tough transmissions, and stout differentials. The obvious became apparent: Take a good tractor and make it better. Jon Kinzenbaw of Williamsburg, Iowa, did this by replacing the factory engine with higher horsepower powerplants.

Numerous modifications were required, but he proved that a Detroit Diesel V-8 or a Cummins six-cylinder inline 850 could be successfully married to the 5010 or 5020. Between 1968 and 1974, Kinzenbaw converted approximately 100 5010s and 5020s to Detroit Diesel V-8s, transforming them into real working tractors for farmers who needed gobs more power.

For the particulars of innovative engineering, here are the Kinzenbaw's comments about his robust modified tractors: "Deere & Company always fussed that I repowered their tractors. But, on the other hand, I gave them credit for having a handy, comfortable tractor to drive that had a heavy transmission and rear-end.

"We split the 5010 or 5020 Wheatland or Row-Crop right at the clutch housing. Then we rebuilt a clutch used in an over-the-road truck that had two clutch disks 14 inches in diameter. We developed this clutch to drive the existing transmission shaft. It also turned the outer shaft to turn the PTO so we could maintain the live PTO. We maintained the original clutch release bearing.

"When we adapted this engine to the original clutch housing we made an adapter plate that accommodated the Detroit Diesel V-8 we installed. Horsepower could range from 275 to 318.

"The Detroit Diesel 8V71 V-8 engine had a round Number 2 bell housing. We adapted that with a 1-inch-thick plate that was drilled to fit the John Deere on the back side and the Detroit Diesel V-8 on the front side. That, along with the clutch assembly that accommodated the transmission drive, PTO, and the clutch release bearing, made that engine fit right up like a hand-in-glove."

Modifying the 5010 or 5020 became part of Kinzenbaw's business activities; however, he did some special modifications "just for fun."

"We always wondered why we didn't try a Cummins engine in a 5020. That's why a couple of years ago we took an old 5020 and repowered it with a used 855 Cummins diesel engine," Kinzenbaw said.

He admitted being drawn to the Cummins engine because it had a lot more torque and a lot more horsepower. Kinzenbaw claims he can get between 290 and 450 horsepower from a Cummins, depending on how he modifies it. The longer, bulkier engine also made it much more difficult to install. He only did the one conversion because he didn't think customers would accept a tractor that had to be a foot longer.

"We made the adapter and the clutch a lot like we did on the Detroit Diesel," Kinzenbaw said. "The frame was constructed out of heavier frame material just like with the other model.

"There wasn't room above the engine for an air cleaner, so we had to side-mount it. We also put a side-mounted exhaust on the tractor, plus a Sound-Gard cab from a 4440 tractor. The fiberglass hood came from a John Deere 8850 four-wheel-drive tractor. The fuel tank was hand-built to make it look good and to fit with the hood we had available.

"We felt this modified, 400-horsepower tractor was 50 percent John Deere and 50 percent Cummins and KINZE. That's why for fun we called it a 5050. It's one of a kind and something we don't intend to offer by any means."

Open the door of the battery compartment and there's a lubrication chart on the inside of the door for quick reference. This is similar to today's combines, but was a first in the 8010/8020's day.

Although this tractor went out the door as a yellow-painted industrial 8010, a factory recall to rebuild the transmission and clutch transformed it into an agricultural 8020. John Deere installed a damaged 7020 cab that was converted to fit the tractor, then added a second door for greater convenience. However, it didn't have an identification plate until owners Mike and Rick Hoffman, Richwood, Ohio, called this to the attention of John Deere. Now their 8020 has a serial number on a computerized tag just like on the new tractors being shipped. It's powered by an in-line six-cylinder Detroit Diesel engine. The 8010/8020 has a grease bank, two different hydraulic systems, front wheels that can be shifted in and out to eliminate excessive tire wear on the road, air brakes, and a hydraulic clutch.

The 8010/8020's three-point hitch was heavily and sturdily built, which it had to be to handle a fully mounted eight-bottom plow.

Tractors that didn't bear a four-digit number, but demonstrated New Generation styling, include the three-cylinder 310 and 510, along with the four-cylinder 710. All were produced at Mannheim.

By 1967, Mannheim, or European models, included the 1020, 2020, 820, 920, 1120, 2120, and 3120. They were produced between 1967 and 1969.

The 505 built at the Getafe Works near Madrid, Spain, was the first Deere & Company-designed tractor to be manufactured in Spain. It was introduced in 1963. This was before the worldwide concept, but it still carried some recognizable New Generation family styling features.

In 1966, Spain followed with the 515 and the 717 models. The 818 was added in 1967. These models were all part of the worldwide Deere & Company tractor design effort.

Argentina began producing New Genera-

This tractor has a trio of ways in which it's remarkably unique. First, it's the first four-wheel-drive model ever built and marketed by John Deere. Second, the identification plate attached to it indicates it's the very first 8010 produced. Third, it's the only 8010 that didn't go back on a factory recall for replacement with a more rugged transmission and clutch. This makes it the only 8010 in existence, because the factory-rebuilt 8010s returned as 8020s.

After it was made in 1959, it was shipped to Montana covered with canvas to prevent other manufacturers from seeing what John Deere was up to. It was never sold to a farmer. It returned to the Waterloo, Iowa, plant where it was used for factory yard work.

Serial number 001 is riveted onto this 7020. The 7020 was John Deere's third attempt at providing a four-wheel-drive tractor. The first was the 8010/8020 in 1959. Next, in 1969, came the WA-14 and WA-17 which John Deere sold but didn't manufacture. They had a rated horsepower of 178 and 220 at the drawbar. In 1970, the 7020 was introduced. It offered a variety of wheel adjustments for various row spacing and a three-point hitch. Wheels could be either dual or single, as shown. The narrow hood made sighting down a row easier, yet the 7020 was equally at home in the larger fields of the Plains and the West.

Well, it looks like a New Generation tractor, but then again, it doesn't. Still in its working clothes, this John Deere-Lanz 300 model is powered by a three-cylinder diesel that puts out 30-plus horsepower. The plant in Mannheim, Germany, also produced 200 and 500 model tractors. John Deere bought out Lanz in the late 1950s.

tion-styled tractors in 1970. These included the 1420, 2420, 3420, and 4420 models. Essentially these were the 20 Series tractors with some variations to accommodate the prevailing economic climate. For example, the 1420 ran a three-cylinder 43-horsepower John Deere engine, yet retained its 445 predecessor's five-speed transmission.

The engine of the four-cylinder 2420, similar to the Mannheim 2120, was rated at 66 horsepower. The 3420 used a six-cylinder engine of 77 horsepower that had much of the same specifications as the European 3120. Saran, France, produced the six-

cylinder engines for the 4420. They were rated at 102 horsepower.

These three Argentina tractors used the eight-speed Syncro-Range transmission. The 20 Series was in the line from 1970 to 1975.

Canadian dealers received their smaller Deere & Company tractors from the Dubuque, Iowa, plant until the 710 Mannheim model was introduced. This started a trend that led to the Canadian dealers receiving most of their smaller models from Mannheim, including the 920, 1120, and 2120.

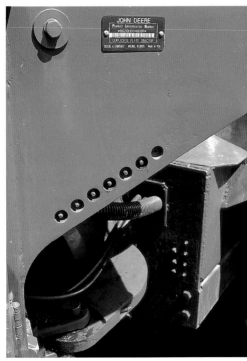

The 8010/8020 was the first Deere & Company tractor to provide the convenience of a grease bank. Everything that needed lubrication on the tractor, except for the universal joints and a couple of hinges, can be greased from this spot. This 8010/8020 didn't receive a new identification plate when it was converted into an 8020. The computerized serial number is recent.

Egging Cab Company installed the cab on this 8010/8020. Although the 8010/8020 predates the release of the New Generation tractors by a year, most "green-blooded" people still consider it part of the New Generation family. One reason is appearance and the other is because it offered so many features never seen before in a tractor.

The 8010/8020's red taillights are set into the fender just as they are on new tractors. When the headlights were on, there was a courtesy light at both sets of steps and another light in the toolbox area.

When an 8010/8020 is throttled up, first there's a dense cloud of smoke from the exhaust pipe, and then there's a surge of power as the wheels dig in and it plunges ahead.

Designed to fill the power requirements of large-acreage grain producers and farmers with heavy tillage requirements, the "8010" Diesel with more than 200 horsepower efficiently handles such big-capacity equipment as a 2-1/2-ton 8-bottom integral moldboard plow, a 3-ton "pickup" offset disk harrow and 46 feet of drawn field cultivators.

With the 10-ton, four-wheel-drive "8010" a fleet owner can retire up to three 6-plow tractors and their operators. "8010" fuel savings are outstanding, too—in recent tests an "8010" with a 31-foot tool carrier covered 19 acres an hour at a cost of only 6 cents per acre. Here is truly power for profit . . . power to speed jobs to an early completion.

The "8010" Diesel features two sections, called "bogies," connected by a flexible coupling which permits units to "bend" and rotate in relation to each other.

QUALITY FEATURES

Two-Bogie Chassis Design
Excellent stability, flexibility and safety are offered by the "8010" Diesel's two-bogie chassis design. A 16-degree range of oscillation between front and rear units enables the "8010" to cross rough ground, climb over obstacles and work in uneven ground with ease and safety . . . even on a 30-degree tilt.

Powerful 6-Cylinder Engine
A General Motors 2-cycle, 6-cylinder Diesel engine delivers more than 200 engine horsepower and provides 9,000 to 11,000 pounds of pull at the drawbar for normal operations . . . in excess of 20,000 pounds maximum pull.

Four-Wheel Drive
Four-wheel drive is provided for field operation. For use on the highway, the "8010" can be converted to two-wheel drive by means of a front-axle disconnect lever.

Compact Design
The "8010" features a compact design and rubber-tired carriage permitting highway operation and offering greater maneuverability in the field.

Ruggedly Built Transmission
Nine forward speeds ranging from 2 to 18 mph are provided by the "8010" Diesel's ruggedly built transmission.

Powerful Hydraulic System
A choice of 2- or 3-circuit hydraulic systems is offered. Each circuit is double-acting and independent of the others. "Floating" action is provided.

Heavy-Duty 3-Point Hitch
Owners can attach and detach tools rapidly . . . transport large equipment quickly from field to field . . . and efficiently utilize 2- to 3-ton hitch-mounted implements with the heavy-duty 3-Point Hitch of the "8010."

Power Steering
Steering is accomplished by a powerful hydraulic cylinder or ram located in the forward bogie. This cylinder "bends" the bogies together in the direction of the turn. Turning radius is only 17-1/2 feet, and turns can be accomplished under full power with large-capacity implements in the ground.

10-25-1

Everybody needs a hobby, and, the hobby of Paul Kleiber of Plymouth, Wisconsin, is big iron, really big iron. He restores and collects 8010/8020 tractors. All five of these 8010/8020 tractors were built in 1960. John Deere later recalled all the 8010s to rebuild their transmissions and clutches. The tractors were returned carrying 8020 decals. Kleiber reports that his 8010/8020s are extremely smooth-running tractors and that their hydraulic clutches make them especially easy to shift. Roughly half of the 8010/8020s came with Category 5 three-point hitches.

This is the biggie, the 8010 Diesel tractor. According to this page concerning its many features, each of the tractor's swiveling two sections is called a "bogie."

THE IMPORTANCE OF SUPPORT LITERATURE

There's an interesting facet of tractor production that's seldom, if ever, considered: the invaluable support literature.

Think for a moment about all the sales and promotional literature, owner manuals, and shop manuals that must be written, printed, and distributed for each tractor model that goes out the factory door.

In the case of the New Generation tractors this was literally a blank sheet of paper effort, too. Every specification, every feature, and every service procedure had to be identified and written in clear, concise language. In this case, there was no existing material to rewrite or update.

Photographs and illustrations were both desirable and necessary and had to be produced from scratch. And once content was agreed on, all the material had to be attractively printed, bound, and delivered.

Through the course of the New Generation's life, millions of pieces of literature and manuals were printed. A large percentage of these ultimately found their way into the hands of consumers. Keep in mind that in the publishing industry, a work that "sells" millions of copies is considered to be a runaway best seller.

Fred Hileman was the Deere & Company employee given the responsibility for developing all the support literature required for the New Generation tractors. He relates that initially due to the volume of work involved the decision was made to contract with an outside firm to do the work.

This was done; however, shortly after the task began the decision was reversed, possibly because of security concerns. Hileman was informed that he now had to finish the job.

He protested that he had no writers, no photographers, no illustrators. He was told to "get them." He did, and he also got a new facility in which to house the project. He recalls that the design for the tractors was set in 1958. This gave him and his new staff only two years to write and produce all the necessary support material.

Incidentally, when each dealer arrived back at his John Deere store after attending the "D-Day" introduction in Dallas, Texas, he found boxes containing the complete literature concerning the New Generation tractors awaiting him.

To be sure, a close study of this material may reveal that there are minor inconsistencies in model types. This could be due to work done partly by the contracted company, or it could be the result of different nomenclature used between the Waterloo and Dubuque plants.

A case in point is the model designations. Some tractors are called "Standard" one place and "Utility" in another. "Row-Crop" is another designation that tends to confuse people. Here's a general guideline to the options that could provide many different configurations. An alpha-code used for manufacturing identification purposes uses capital letters inside parentheses.

Row-Crop Tractor (R): Tricycle front wheels or single front wheel

Row-Crop Utility Tractor (RU): Has an adjustable wide front axle

Utility Tractor (U): Has a wide front axle

Low Utility Tractor (LU): Underslung exhaust system, wide front axle

High Utility Tractor (HU): More clearance underneath, wide front axle

Hi-Crop Tractor (H): Extra high clearance, wide front axle

Special Row-Crop Utility Tractor (RUS): Economical version of the Row-Crop Utility with smaller shell fenders, a steel seat, and manual steering

Grove and Orchard Tractor (O): Low Utility fitted with special fenders and other metal work to keep tree limbs from catching on the tractor

Standard Tractor: Same as a Utility Tractor

Agricultural Crawler Tractor (CA): Track-laying tractor painted green and yellow like agricultural tractors

Industrial Crawler (C): Track-laying tractor painted yellow

Industrial Wheel Tractor (W): Industrial model of agricultural tractor painted yellow

Wheel Forklift (F): Uses components of wheel tractors and is painted yellow. There were also a few crawler versions of the forklift.

APPENDICES

Note: The Deere & Company production year doesn't run concurrently with the company's fiscal year or calendar year. Neither does the production year have a set date for its start or end, which can be shorter or longer than 12 months.

Serial numbers for some tractors haven't yet been transferred to a computer database. To tabulate these serial numbers it's necessary to physically go through the serial number register and count numbers. Although this list isn't infallible, it's the best information now available.

The serial number listed in the left column designates the first production machine for a particular year. The following year's serial number is the first machine built in that year. Therefore, the numbers in between approximately represent one year's production.

New Generation Serial Number System

Serial Numbers	Year	Serial Numbers	Year	Serial Numbers	Year	Serial Numbers	Year
1010		**2020**		**4010**		**6030**	
10001	1961	14502	1965	1000	1961	33000	1972
23630	1962	14680	1966	20200	1962	33550	1973
32188	1963	42721	1967	38200	1963	34586	1974
43900	1964	65176	1968			35400	1975
53722	1965	82404	1969	**4020**		36014	1976
		102032	1970	65000	1964	36577	1977
1010 Crawler		117500	1971	91000	1965		
10001	1960			119000	1966	**7020**	
13692	1961	**2510**		145660	1967	1000	1971
23630	1962	1000	1966	173982	1968	2006	1972
32301	1963	8958	1967	201000	1969	2700	1973
42101	1964	14291	1968	222143	1970	3156	1974
52722	1965			250000	1971	3579	1975
		2520		260791	1972		
1020		17000	1969			**7520**	
14501	1965	19416	1970	**4320**		1000	1972
14682	1966	22000	1971	6000	1971	1600	1973
42715	1967	22911	1972	17031	1972	3054	1974
65184	1968	23865	1973			4945	1975
82409	1969			**4520**			
102038	1970	**3010**		1000	1969	**8010**	
117500	1971	1000	1961	7005	1970	1000	1961
134700	1972	19416	1962				
157109	1973	32400	1963	**4620**		**8020**	
				10000	1971	1000	1964
2010		**3020**	.	13692	1972		
10001	1961	50000	1964			**820**	
21087	1962	68000	1965	**5010**		10000	1968
31250	1963	84000	1966	1000	1963	23100	1969
44036	1964	97286	1967	4500	1964	36000	1970
58186	1965	112933	1968	8000	1965	54000	1971
		123000	1969			71850	1972
2010 Crawler		129897	1970	**5020**		90200	1973
26001	1962	150000	1971	12000	1966		
31271	1963	154197	1972	15650	1967	**1520**	
44168	1964			20399	1968	76112	1968
58186	1965	**4000**		24038	1969	82405	1969
		211422	1969	26624	1970	102061	1970
		222143	1970	30000	1971	117500	1971
		250000	1971	30608	1972	134700	1972
		260791	1972			157109	1973

New Generation Production

Models	Production Years	Location
1010:	1961–1965	Dubuque, Iowa
2010:	1961–1965	Dubuque, Iowa
3010:	1961–1963	Waterloo, Iowa
4010:	1961–1963	Waterloo, Iowa
5010:	1963–1965	Waterloo, Iowa
3020:	1964–1972	Waterloo, Iowa
4020:	1964–1972	Waterloo, Iowa
1020:	1965–1973	Dubuque, Iowa
2020:	1965–1971	Dubuque, Iowa
2510:	1966–1968	Waterloo, Iowa
5020:	1966–1972	Waterloo, Iowa
1520:	1968–1973	Dubuque, Iowa
2520:	1969–1973	Waterloo, Iowa
4000:	1969–1972	Waterloo, Iowa
4520:	1969–1970	Waterloo, Iowa
4320:	1971–1972	Waterloo, Iowa
4620:	1971–1972	Waterloo, Iowa
7020:	1971–1975	Waterloo, Iowa
6030:	1972–1977	Waterloo, Iowa
7520:	1972–1975	Waterloo, Iowa
8010:	1959 only	Waterloo, Iowa
820:	1968–1973	Waterloo, Iowa, and Mannheim, Germany

Tractor Specifications

Note: The information below is offered only as a general guide. Although it may be accurate for a specific model in a specific year, it's not intended as complete material for all models and all years.

1010 Single Row-Crop Tractor

Horsepower: 35 (PTO maximum factory-observed at maximum engine speed—2,500 rpm)
Shipping Weight: Approximately 3,085 pounds
Engine: Vertical, four-cylinder, valve-in-head, four-stroke cycle
    Operating speed range: 1,500 to 2,500 rpm

	Gasoline	Diesel
Bore and stroke (inches):	3 1/2x3	3 5/8x3 1/2
Compression ratio:	7.6 to 1	19 to 1
Displacement (cubic inches):	115.45	144.8

    Lubrication: Pressure system with bypass-type oil filter
    Cooling: Pressurized with water pump, thermostat, and fixed bypass
Power Take-Off: Standard equipment-transmission-driven 540 rpm (PTO stub shaft extra), special equipment-independent "live" 540–1,000 rpm, with hand-lever clutch
Clutch: Foot-operated automotive-type with single 10-inch plate
Brakes: Self-energizing disk type, foot-operated individually or simultaneously
Electrical System: 12-volt battery with generator and starter
Hydraulic System: Special equipment: single or dual hydraulic system, remote cylinder control
Capacities
    Cooling system: 3 gallons
    Fuel tank (gasoline and diesel): 12 gallons
    Engine lubrication, including filter: 5 quarts
    Transmission: 2 gallons
Standard Equipment: Oil pressure indicator light; generator charge indicator light; water temperature gauge; 12-volt dry-charge battery (56 amp, gasoline—85 amp, Diesel); electric starter and generator; fenders; key starter switch; adjustable front axle; glow plugs (diesel); speed-hour meter; transmission-driven power take-off (less stub shaft)
Optional Equipment: Gasoline or diesel engine; manual or power steering; regular or deluxe seat; vertical or horizontal muffler; manually adjusted or power-adjusted rear wheels
Special Equipment: Three-point hitch (Category 1), with Load-and-Depth Control; ASAE-SAE standard swinging drawbar; PTO stub shaft; single or dual hydraulic system; remote cylinder; remote cylinder control; front-end weights; rear-wheel weights; rear-wheel spacers; lights; belt pulley; fuel gauge; cigarette lighter; precleaner; muffler cover; seat arm cushions

1010 Utility Tractor

Horsepower: 35 (PTO maximum factory-observed at maximum engine speed—2,500 rpm)
Shipping Weight: Approximately 3,035 pounds
Engine: Vertical, four-cylinder, valve-in-head, four-stroke cycle
    Operating speed range: 1,500 to 2,500 rpm

	Gasoline	Diesel
Bore and stroke (inches):	3 1/2x3	3 5/8x3 1/2
Compression ratio:	7.6 to 1	19 to 1
Displacement (cubic inches):	115.45	144.48

    Lubrication: Pressure system with bypass-type oil filter
    Cooling: Pressurized with water pump, thermostat, and fixed bypass
Power Take-Off: Standard equipment-transmission-driven 540 rpm (stub shaft extra), special equipment-independent "live" 540 to 1,000 rpm, with hand-lever clutch
Clutch: Foot-operated automotive-type with single 10-inch plate
Brakes: Self-energizing disk-type, foot-operated individually or simultaneously
Electrical System: 12-volt battery with generator and starter
Hydraulic System: Special equipment: single hydraulic system; remote cylinder control
Capacities
    Cooling system: 3 gallons
    Fuel tank (gasoline and diesel): 12 gallons
    Engine lubrication, including filter: 5 quarts
    Transmission: 2 gallons
Standard Equipment: Oil pressure indicator light; generator charge indicator light; water temperature gauge; 12-volt dry-charge battery (56 amps, gasoline; 85 amps, diesel); electric starter and generator; fenders; key starter switch; adjustable front axle; glow plugs (diesel); speed-hour meter; transmission-driven 540 rpm power take-off (less stub shaft)
Optional Equipment: Gasoline or diesel engine; manual or power steering; regular or deluxe seat; vertical or horizontal muffler; underneath exhaust; manually adjusted or power-adjusted rear wheels; transmission-driven or independent PTO
Special Equipment: Three-point hitch (Category 1) with Load-and-Depth Control; ASAE-SAE standard swinging drawbar; single hydraulic system; PTO stub shaft; remote cylinder; remote cylinder control; front-end weight; rear-wheel weight; rear-wheel spacers; lights; belt pulley; fuel gauge; cigarette lighter; precleaner; muffler cover; seat arm cushions

1010 Agricultural Crawler Tractor

Horsepower: 35 (PTO maximum factory-observed at maximum engine speedÑ2,500 rpm)
Shipping Weight: Approximately 4,600 pounds
Engine: Vertical, four-cylinder, valve-in-head, four-stroke cycle
    Operating speed range: 1,500 to 2,500 rpm

	Gasoline	Diesel
Bore and stroke (inches):	3 1/2x3	3 5/8x3 1/2
Compression ratio:	7.62 to 1	19 to 1
Displacement (cubic inches):	115.45	144.48

    Lubrication: Pressure system with bypass-type oil filter
    Cooling: Pressurized with water pump, thermostat, and fixed bypass
Power Take-Off: Transmission-driven, 540 rpm (stubshaft extra)
Clutch: 11-inch single disk, foot-operated
Electrical System: 12-volt battery with generator and starter
Hydraulic System: Special equipment, single or double, for one or two remote cylinders
Steering
    Clutches: Multiple disk
    Brakes: Contracting bond
Track and Track Frame
    Track frame: 4- or 5-roller
    Track shoes (types and sizes): All-purpose semi-grouser, 12-inch. Steel grouser, 10-, 12-, or 14-inch. Snow shoes, 12- or 14-inch. Rubber, 10-inch
Dimensions
    Height to top of hood: 53 5/16 inches
    Overall height: 60 inches
    Overall width: 61 1/8 inches
    Overall length (measured at tracks): 102 1/8 inches
    Clearance (at rear round bar): 21 5/1 6 inches
Capacities
    Cooling system: 2 1/2 gallons
    Fuel tank (gasoline and diesel): 12 gallons
    Crankcase, including filter: 6 quarts
    Transmission: 2 1/4 gallons
    Final drive cases, each: 2 pints
Standard Equipment: Oil pressure indicator light; generator charge indicator light; water temperature gauge; electric starter and generator; 12-volt dry-charge battery; platform and fenders; heavy-duty front bottom plate; key starter switch; four-speed transmission; exhaust muffler cover (diesel); rock guards (five-roller);

fuel gauge; fuel filter; air cleaner; track tension adjuster (manual); manual steering—brake-clutch unit; tachometer

Optional Equipment: Gasoline or diesel engine; deluxe or regular seat; four- or five-roller track assembly, or four-roller with oversize front idler; choice of type and size track shoes; horizontal or vertical muffler; regular or notched-type drive sprockets; dry-charge battery (56- or 85-amp—85 standard on diesel)

Special Equipment: Universal three-point hitch; Quik-Coupler; single or dual hydraulic system, with controls; breakaway couplings; remote hydraulic cylinder; power take-off assembly; belt pulley assembly; heavy-duty rear bottom plate; auxiliary air cleaner (pre-cleaner); seat side arm cushions; caulks for all-purpose semigrouser shoes; electric light (front, rear, panel, and warning light plug-in socket); electric hour meter; cigarette lighter; exhaust muffler cover (gasoline); front hitch; rock guards (four-roller); hydraulic track tension adjuster (five-roller); drawbar

2010 Row-Crop Tractor

Horsepower: 45 (PTO maximum factory-observed at maximum engine speed—2,500 rpm)
Shipping Weight: Approximately 4,600 pounds
Engine: Vertical, four-cylinder, valve-in-head, four-stroke cycle
Operating speed range: 1,500 to 2,500 rpm

	Gasoline	LP-Gas	Diesel
Bore and stroke (inches):	3 5/8x3 1/2	3 5/8x3 1/2	3 7/8x3 1/2
Compression ratio:	7.6 to 1	8.9 to 1	19 to 1
Displacement (cubic inches):	145	145	165

Lubrication: Pressure system with bypass-type oil filter
Cooling: Pressurized with water pump, thermostat, and fixed bypass

Power Take-Off: Special equipment. Independent, engine-driven, rear, with hand-lever clutch; provides dual speeds of 540 and 1,000 rpm
Clutch: Foot-operated, spring-loaded, dry disk
Brakes: Self-energizing disk type, foot-operated individually or simultaneously
Electrical System: 12-volt battery with generator and starter
Hydraulic System: Special equipment: single or dual, front rockshaft, remote cylinder control

Capacities
Cooling system: 3 gallons
Fuel tank (gasoline and diesel): 18 gallons
Fuel tank (LP gas): 22.6 gallons (80 percent full)
Engine lubrication, including filter: 5 quarts
Transmission-hydraulic system: 8 gallons

Standard Equipment: Indicator light for generator; indicator light for oil pressure; water temperature gauge; key switch with safety start; 12-volt starter; generator; hydraulic pump; transmission oil filter; lights; oil wash air cleaner; electric outlet socket; liquid-level fuel gauge, filler valves, electric fuel shutoff (LP gas); fuel filter (diesel and gasoline); fuel shutoff control (diesel); glow plugs (diesel); speed-hour meter

Optional Equipment: Gasoline, diesel, or LP gas engine; manual or power steering; regular or deluxe seat; 56- or 85-ampere battery (12-volt, dry-charge); conventional dual wheels, Roll-O-Matic dual wheels, wide adjustable front axle, or single front wheel; manually adjusted or power-adjusted rear wheels; vertical muffler or tailpipe and muffler; choice of tire sizes and types as listed; front-mounted lights; fender-mounted lights; combination front- and fender-mounted lights; dual fender-mounted lights

Special Equipment: Single or dual hydraulic system; front rockshaft; Universal Three-Point Hitch; Quik-Coupler; single remote cylinder control; remote cylinder with flexible oil lines; independent "live" 540–1,000 rpm power take-off; belt pulley; foot throttle; front-end weight; rear wheel weights; fuel gauge (gasoline and diesel); cigarette lighter; cover for vertical muffler; auxiliary battery with box (diesel); drawbar; implement attachment brackets

2010 Row-Crop Utility Tractor

Horsepower: 45 (PTO maximum factory-observed at maximum engine speed—2,500 rpm)
Shipping Weight: Approximately 4,600 pounds
Engine: Vertical, four-cylinder, valve-in-head, four-stroke cycle
Operating speed range: 1,500 to 2,500 rpm

	Gasoline	LP Gas	Diesel
Bore and stroke (inches):	3 5/8x3 1/2	3 5/8x3 1/2	3 7/8x3 1/2
Compression ratio:	7.6 to 1	8.9 to 1	19 to 1
Displacement (cubic inches):	145	145	165

Lubrication: Pressure system with bypass-type oil filter
Cooling: Pressurized with water pump, thermostat, and fixed bypass

Power Take-Off: Special equipment. Independent, engine-driven, rear, with hand-lever clutch; provides dual speeds of 540 and 1,000 rpm

Clutch: Foot-operated, spring-loaded, dry disk
Brakes: Self-energizing disk type, foot-operated individually or simultaneously
Electrical System: 12-volt battery with generator and starter
Hydraulic System: Special equipment: single or dual hydraulic system, front rockshaft control for remote cylinder

Capacities
Cooling system: 3 gallons
Fuel tank (gasoline and diesel): 18 gallons
Fuel tank (LP gas): 22.6 gallons (80 percent full)
Engine lubrication, including filter: 5 quarts
Transmission-hydraulic system: 8 gallons

Standard Equipment: Indicator light for generator; indicator light for oil pressure; water temperature gauge; key switch with safety start; 12-volt starter and generator; fenders; hydraulic pump; transmission oil filter; toolbox; oil wash air cleaner; electric outlet socket; liquid-level fuel gauge, filler valves, electric fuel shutoff (LP gas only); fuel filter (diesel and gasoline); fuel shutoff control (diesel); glow plugs (diesel); speed-hour meter

Optional Equipment: Gasoline, diesel, or LP gas engine; manual or power steering; regular or deluxe seat; 56- or 85-amp battery (12-volt, dry-charge); straight or swept-back front axle; disk type or power-adjusted rear wheels; vertical muffler or tailpipe and muffler; choice of tire sizes and types as listed

Special Equipment: Single or dual hydraulic system; front rockshaft; Universal Three-Point Hitch; Quik-Coupler; single remote cylinder control; remote cylinder with flexible oil lines; power take-off assembly; belt pulley assembly; foot throttle; front-end weight; rear wheel weights; lighting equipment; fuel gauge (gasoline and diesel); cigarette lighter; cover for vertical muffler; frame side plates; high-altitude cylinder head; auxiliary battery with box (diesel); canvas-type operator cab; drawbar; implement attachment brackets

2010 Hi-Crop Tractor

Horsepower: Maximum observed on power take-off
Diesel: 46.67 (Nebraska Test No. 799)
Gasoline: 46.86 (Nebraska Test No. 800)
LP Gas: Approximately 45, factory observed (not tested at Nebraska)
Shipping Weight: Gas: approximately 5,345; diesel: approximately 5,460
Engine

	Gasoline	LP Gas	Diesel
Bore and stroke (inches):	3 5/8x3 1/2	3 5/8x3 1/2	3 7/8x3 1/2
Compression ratio:	7.6 to 1	8.9 to 1	19 to 1
Displacement (cubic inches):	145	145	165

Lubrication: Pressure system with bypass-type oil filter
Cooling: Pressurized with water pump, thermostat, and fixed bypass

Power Take-Off: Special equipment: independent, engine-driven, rear, with hand-lever clutch; provides dual speeds of 540 and 1,000 rpm
Clutch: Foot-operated, spring-loaded, dry disk
Brakes: Self-energizing disk-type, foot-operated individually or simultaneously
Electrical System: 12-volt battery with generator and starter
Hydraulic System: Special equipment: single or dual system; front rockshaft; remote cylinder control

Capacities
Cooling system: 3 gallons
Fuel tank (gasoline and diesel): 16 gallons
Fuel tank (LP gas): 22.6 gallons (80 percent full)
Engine lubrication, including filter: 5 quarts
Transmission-hydraulic system: 8 gallons

Standard Equipment: Indicator light for generator; indicator light for oil pressure; water temperature gauge; key switch with safety start; 12-volt electric starter and generator; mounting step; hydraulic pump; transmission oil filter; liquid-level fuel gauge, filler valves, electric fuel shutoff (LP gas only); fuel filter (diesel and gasoline); fuel-shutoff control (diesel); glow plugs (diesel); toolbox; oil-wash air cleaner; electrical outlet socket; lights; speed-hour meter

Optional Equipment: Gasoline, diesel, or LP gas engine; manual or power steering; regular or deluxe seat; 56- or 85-amp battery (12-volt, dry-charge); choice of tire sizes, plies, and types as listed; adjustable rear wheels; vertical muffler or tailpipe and muffler

Special Equipment: Single or dual hydraulic system; front rockshaft; Universal Three-Point Hitch; Quik-Coupler; remote cylinder with flexible oil lines; single remote cylinder control; power take-off; belt pulley; foot throttle; front-end weight; rear wheel weights; front-mounted lights; fuel gauge (gasoline and diesel); cigarette lighter; cover for vertical muffler; implement attachment brackets

1020, 1520, and 2020 Tractors

Horsepower:

	Gasoline	Diesel
1020	38.82	38.92
1520	47.86	46.52
2020	53.91	54.09

Shipping Weight (pounds)

1020	4,210	4,260
1520	4,490	4,550
2020	5,500	5,580

Engine: Vertical, valve-in-head, four-stroke cycle
1020 and 1520: three-cylinder
2020: four-cylinder
Operating speed range: 1,500 to 2,500 rpm

Bore and stroke (inches)	Gasoline	Diesel
1020 and 2020	3 7/8x3 3/8	3 7/8x4 5/16
1520	4x4 1/3	4x4 1/3
Displacement (cubic inches)		
1020	135	152
1520	164	164
2020	180	202
Compression ratio		
1020 and 2020	7.5 to 1	16.3 to 1
1520	8 to 1	16.3 to 1

Lubrication: Pressure system with full-flow oil filter
Cooling: Pressurized with water pump, thermostat, and fixed bypass

Capacities

Cooling system	
1020	2 3/4 gallons
1520	3 gallons
2020	3 gallons
Fuel tank	
1020	16 1/2 gallons
1520	19 1/2 gallons
2020	19 1/2 gallons

Engine lubrication, including filter: 6 quarts
Transmission and hydraulic system: 10 gallons

Power Take-Off: Transmission-driven 540 rpm (1020 only). Independent or continuous "live" 540 rpm. Independent or continuous "live" 540 to 1,000 rpm. Mid-"live" 1,000 rpm. Independent or continuous "live" 540 rear with mid-1,000. Independent or continuous "live" 540–1,000 rear with mid-1,000

Clutch: Automotive-type single or dual stage

Brakes: Hydraulic; foot-operated individually or simultaneously; disks operate in cooled oil

Hydraulic System: Closed center rockshaft, one or two independent rear outlets for double-acting remote cylinder

Base Equipment: Three- or four-cylinder engine; constant-mesh transmissions—eight forward, four reverse selections; 12-volt starter and electrical system; alternator; transistorized voltage regulator; key ignition switch with safety start; closed-center hydraulic system; 13-gallon per minute pump; continuous "live" 540-rpm rear PTO; rockshaft; three-point hitch with solid draft links; Category 1 with sway chains on 1020, Category 2 with sway blocks on 1520 and 2020; 41-amp, dry-charge battery (gasoline); 70-amp, dry-charge battery (diesel); fenders with lights; manual steering on 1020 and 1520; power steering on 2020; vertical muffler; air cleaner (oil-bath type); cushion seat; speed-hour meter; fuel gauge; hand throttle adjustable front axle; oil-pressure and alternator-charge indicator lights; water-temperature gauge; eight-position adjustable steel wheels (RU, LU); eight-position cast wheels (HU) antifreeze; exhaust muffler cover on upright mufflers; and swinging drawbar

Special Equipment*: Differential lock, foot-engaged power take-off—rear; transmission-driven 540 on 1020 only; continuous "live" 540–1,000; independent "live" 540; independent "live" 540–1,000; mid-1,000 single or dual remote-cylinder controls with regular or breakaway couples; remote cylinder; three-point hitch with telescoping draft links; front-end and rear-wheel weights; cigarette lighter; precleaner and ether starting aid for diesels; power steering for 1020 and 1520; toolbox below water heater; deluxe seat with shock absorber; 70-amp battery (gasoline); 140-amp (two 70-amp) batteries (gasoline or diesel); foot throttle; heavy cast wheels; rack-and-pinion rear wheels; power-adjusted rear wheels; sweptback front axle; dry air-cleaner with restriction indicator; side frames; high-altitude engine; Roll-Gard with seatbelt; canopy top for Roll-Gard; Hi-Lo Shift transmission; direction-reverse transmission; 88-inch wide front axle; tractor step for 38-inch tires

* Some options apply only to certain models.

Attachments for Field Installation: Electrical plug-in socket; belt pulley; rear-axle extension—increases wheel tread 8 inches; weather shield; hitch drawbar; Quik-Coupler for Category 2 three-point hitch

1020 Orchard

Horsepower: 38.82 gasoline, 38.92 diesel. Official test figures observed PTO at 2,500 rpm
Engine: Vertical, three-cylinder, valve-in-head, four-stroke
Speed ranges: Governed: 600 to 2,500; operating: 1,500 to 2,500

	Gasoline	Diesel
Bore and stroke (inches):	3 7/8x3 7/8	3 7/8x4 5/16
Compression ratio:	7.5 to 1	16.3 to 1
Displacement (cubic inches):	135	152

Lubrication: Pressure system with full-flow oil filter
Cooling: Pressurized with water pump, thermostat, and fixed bypass

Power Take-Off: Transmission-driven rear 540 rpm; or rear "live" 540 rpm; or rear "live" combination 540–1,000 rpm; or midpoint "live" 1,000 rpm
Engine Clutch: Automotive-type single or dual stage
Brakes: Hydraulic; foot-operated; disk type
Electrical System: 12-volt starter; alternator; transistorized voltage regulator; key ignition with safety start
Instrument Panel: Speed-hour meter; oil pressure indicator light; alternator charge indicator light; water temperature gauge; fuel gauge
Hydraulic System: Hydraulic pump, 13 gallons per minute. Special equipment, single or dual remote cylinder control with breakaway couplers

Capacities
Cooling system: 2 3/4 gallons
Crankcase: 6 quarts
Transmission: 10 gallons
Fuel tank: 16 1/2 gallons

1520 Orchard

Horsepower: 47.86 gasoline and 46.52 diesel. Official test figures observed at PTO at 2,500 rpm
Engine: Vertical, three-cylinder, valve-in-head, four-stroke
Speed ranges: Governed: 600 to 2,500; operating: 1,500 to 2,500

	Gasoline	Diesel
Bore and stroke (inches):	4x4 1/3	4x4 1/3
Compression ratio:	8 to 1	16.5 to 1
Displacement (cubic inches):	164	164

Lubrication: Pressure system with full-flow oil filter
Cooling: Pressurized with water pump, thermostat, and fixed bypass

Power Take-Off: Rear "live" 540 rpm; or rear "live" combination 540–1,000 rpm; or midpoint "live" 1,000 rpm
Engine Clutch: Automotive-type dual stage
Brakes: Hydraulic; foot-operated; disk type
Electrical System: 12-volt starter; alternator; transistorized voltage regulator; key ignition with safety start
Instrument Panel: Speed-hour meter; oil pressure indicator light; alternator charge indicator light; water temperature gauge; fuel gauge
Hydraulic System: Hydraulic pump, 13 gallons per minute; special equipment, single or dual remote cylinder control with breakaway couplers

Capacities
Cooling system: 3 gallons
Crankcase: 6 quarts
Transmission: 10 gallons
Fuel tank: 19 1/2 gallons

2010 Agricultural Crawler

Horsepower (at 2500 engine rpm)
Net (with accessories) engine flywheel (corrected factory observed): 52.0
PTO: 47.72
Drawbar: 39.08

Shipping Weight: Approximately 8,492 pounds (with five-roller track frame, 12-inch shoes)
Engine: John Deere, diesel, vertical, four-cylinder, valve-in-head, four-stroke cycle
Bore and stroke: 3 7/8x3 1/2 inches
Compression ratio: 19 to 1
Displacement: 165 cubic inches
Lubrication: Pressure system with bypass-type filter
Cooling: Pressurized with water pump, thermostat, and fixed bypass
Air Cleaner: Oil-wash type

Capacities
Fuel tank: 16 gallons
Cooling system: 3 gallons
Crankcase, including filter: 6 quarts
Transmission: 27 quarts
Final drive cases (each): 1/2 gallon

Power Take-Off: Transmission driven, 1,000 rpm (stub-shaft assembly extra)

Transmission Options

1. Constant Mesh: Four speed ranges; with high, low, and reverse speeds in each range, shifted mechanically
2. H-L-R: Four speed ranges; with high, low, and reverse speeds in each range, shifted hydraulically without clutching

Engine Clutch

1. Tractor with Constant Mesh Transmission: 11-inch, spring-loaded, dry disk, pedal operated
2. Tractor with H-L-R Transmission: 10-inch, spring-loaded, dry disk, hand-lever operated (for cold weather starting)

Hydraulic System: Double system (special equipment)

Steering: Clutch-brake system, multiple disk, 16 friction surfaces per clutch

Brakes: Contracting band

Electrical System: 12-volt with generator

Starter: 12-volt electric starter

Track and Track Frame

Track Rollers, each side:
  Number: 5
  Diameter: 7 3/16 inches
  Type of bearings: Bronze
Upper Support Idler, each side:
  Number: 1
  Diameter: 4 7/8 inches
  Type of bearings: Bronze
Track shoes (type and sizes): Grouser 10-, 12-, or 14-inch; open-center grouser, 12- or 14-inch; all-purpose semigrouser, 12-inch; snow shoes, 12- or 14-inch; rubber, 10-inch (all full-hardened except 10-inch grouser)
Track pins diameter: 1 inch
Track pin bushing diameter: 1 9/16 inch
Number of track shoes, each side: 39
Total ground contact area: 10-inch shoes, 1,445 square inches; 12-inch shoes, 1,734 square inches; 14-inch shoes, 2,023 square inches
Ground pressure: 14-inch shoes (pound per square inch), 4.1
Length of track on ground: 72 1/4 inches
Track gauge: 48 inches
Adjustment options: manual or hydraulic

2020 Orchard

Horsepower: 53.91 gasoline and 54.09 diesel; official test figures observed at PTO at 2,500 rpm

Engine: Vertical, four-cylinder, valve-in-head, four-stroke
  Speed ranges: Governed: 600 to 2,500; operating: 1,500 to 2,500

	Gasoline	Diesel
Bore and stroke (inches):	3 7/8x3 7/8	3 7/8x4 5/16
Compression ratio:	7.5 to 1	16.3 to 1
Displacement (cubic inches):	180	202

  Lubrication: Pressure system with full-flow oil filter
  Cooling: Pressurized with water pump, thermostat, and fixed bypass

Power Take-Off: Rear "live" 540 rpm; or rear "live" combination 540 to 1,000 rpm; or mid-point "live" 1,000 rpm

Engine Clutch: Automotive-type single or dual stage

Brakes: Hydraulic; foot-operated; disk type

Electrical System: 12-volt starter; alternator; transistorized voltage regulator; key ignition with safety start

Instrument Panel: Speed-hour meter; oil pressure indicator light; alternator charge indicator light; water temperature gauge; fuel gauge

Hydraulic System: Hydraulic pump, 13 gallons per minute; special equipment, single or dual remote cylinder control with breakaway couplers

Capacities

Cooling system: 3 gallons
Crankcase: 6 quarts
Transmission: 10 gallons
Fuel tank: 19 1/2 gallons

2020 Grove and Orchard

Horsepower: 54 at 2,500 rpm (maximum factory observed at PTO)

Engine: Vertical, four-cylinder, valve-in-head, four-stroke
  Speed ranges: Governed 600 to 2,500, operating 1,500 to 2,500

	Gasoline	Diesel
Bore and stroke (inches):	3 7/8x3 7/8	3 7/8x4 5/16
Compression ratio:	7.5 to 1	16.3 to 1
Displacement (cubic inches):	180	202

Lubrication: Pressure system with full-flow oil filter

Cooling: Pressurized with water pump, thermostat, and fixed bypass

Power Take-Off: Rear "live" 540 rpm, or dual speed 540–1,000 rpm

Engine Clutch: Hand-operated, automotive-type

Brakes: Hydraulic; foot-operated; disk type

Electrical System: 12-volt starter; alternator; transistorized voltage regulator; key ignition with safety start

Instrument Panel: Speed-hour meter; oil pressure indicator light; alternator charge indicator light; water temperature gauge; fuel gauge

Hydraulic System: Hydraulic pump, 13 gallons per minute; single remote cylinder control with breakaway couplers

Capacities

Cooling system: 3 gallons
Crankcase: 6 quarts
Transmission: 10 gallons
Fuel tank: 19 1/2 gallons

2510 Row-Crop Tractor

Horsepower

	Gasoline	Diesel
Syncro-Range	53.74	54.96
Power Shift	49.57	50.66

Shipping Weight: Gas, 5,950 pounds; diesel, 6,100 pounds

Engine: Four-cylinder, wet-sleeve, valve-in-head, variable-speed
  Speed ranges: Governed, 800 to 2,500 rpm; operating, 1,500 to 2,500 rpm

	Gasoline	Diesel
Bore and stroke (inches):	3.86x3.86	3.86x4.33
Compression ratios:	7.5 to 1	16.3 to 1
Displacement (cubic inches):	180.4	202.7

  Lubrication: Full-pressure, full-flow with bypass relief valve, replaceable micronic paper element
  Cooling: Bypass cooling system with centrifugal pump and thermostatic heat control

Capacities (gas and diesel)

Fuel tank: 26 gallons
Cooling system: 3.5 gallons
Crankcase: 6 quarts
Transmission, differential and hydraulic systems:
  Syncro-Range: 8 gallons
  Power Shift: 11 gallons

Power Take-Off: Independent dual-speed rear PTO (540 1,000 rpm at 2,100 rpm engine speed); front power take-off for 1,000-rpm equipment

Clutch: Foot clutch, 11-inch dry-disk type, spring loaded; power shift is multiple wet-disk type

Brakes: Hydraulic power brakes; wet-disk type

Electrical system: 12-volt lighting and accessories, 12-volt starting

Instrument panel: Speed-hour meter; electric fuel gauge, oil pressure, and alternator indicators; coolant temperature gauge; light switch; safety key master and push-button starter switch; cigar lighter. Transmission oil pressure and temperature gauges on Power Shift models

---

2520 Row-Crop Tractors

Horsepower

	Gasoline	Diesel
Syncro-Range:	60.16	61.29
Power Shift:	56.98	56.28

  Maximum observed horsepower measured at the PTO at 2,500 engine rpm in official tests

Shipping Weight: Gas, 6,450 pounds; diesel, 6,600 pounds (with equipment for average field service)

Engine: Four cylinder, variable-speed, wet-sleeve, valve-in-head
  Speed range: Governed, 800 to 2,500 rpm; operating, 1,500 to 2,500 rpm; maximum transport speed, 2.500 rpm

	Gasoline	Diesel
Bore and stroke (inches):	3.86x4.33	4.02x4.33
Compression ratio:	7.6 to 1	16.3 to 1
Displacement (cubic inches):	202.7	219.4

  Lubrication: Full-pressure, full-flow filtration with bypass; micronic paper element
  Cooling: Pressure with centrifugal pump and thermostatic heat control
  Air cleaner: Dry-type with restriction indicator

Capacities (gas and diesel)

Fuel tank: 26 gallons
Cooling system: 14 quarts
Crankcase (includes filter): 7 quarts
Transmission, differential, and hydraulic system (at service intervals)

Syncro-Range: 8 gallons
Power Shift: 11 gallons

Power Take-Off: Independent 540–1,000 rpm rear; 1,000 rpm midpoint; hydraulic-assist dry-disk on Syncro-Range; hydraulic, multiple wet-disk on Power Shift

Transmission: Syncro-Range: Constant-mesh, helical-gears, range-synchronized; 8 forward, 2 reverse. Power Shift: Multiple wet-disk; hydraulically actuated; 8 forward, 4 reverse

Clutch: Syncro-Range: Foot-operated, spring-loaded, 11-inch dry disk; Power Shift: Multiple wet-disk, foot-operated (not required for shifting); hand-operated, dry-disk engine disconnect

Hydraulics: Closed-center, constant-pressure, variable-displacement system

Steering: Full-power, hydrostatic-type; provision for manual operation

Brakes: Full-power, wet-disk type, foot-operated individually or simultaneously; provision for manual operation

Differential Lock: Foot-operated, multiple wet-disk, hydraulically actuated

Electrical System: 12-volt lighting, accessories and starting alternator

Instrument Panel: Speed-hour meter, fuel gauge, engine temperature gauge, engine oil-pressure light, alternator light, transmission temperature gauge, transmission oil-pressure light (Power Shift), air-cleaner restriction light; light-switch; key start switch; cigar lighter; fiber-optic instrument lighting

---

2520 Hi-Crop

Note: The information below applies to Hi-Crop models specifically

Shipping Weight: Gasoline, 7,075 pounds; diesel, 7,125 pounds (with equipment for average field service)

3010 Series Standard Tractor

Horsepower: 55 horsepower taken at PTO at 2,200 rpm engine speed (factory observed)
Shipping Weight: 6,176 pounds
Engine: Four-cylinder, wet sleeve, valve-in-head
Governed speed range: 600 rpm to 2,200 rpm
Operating speed range: 1,500 rpm to 2,200 rpm
Transport speed range: 2,200 rpm to 2,500 rpm

	Gasoline	LP Gas	Diesel
Bore and stroke (inches):	4x4	4x4	4 1/8x4 3/4
Compression ratios:	7.5 to 1	9.0 to 1	16.4 to 1
Displacement (cubic inches):	201.06	201.06	253.9

Lubrication: Full pressure, full flow with bypass relief valve, replaceable micronic paper element
Cooling: Bypass cooling system with centrifugal pump and thermostatic heat control
Power Take-Off: Independent Dual-Speed Rear PTO (540–1,000 rpm at 1,900 rpm engine speed). Front power take-off for 1,000 rpm equipment

Capacities
Fuel Tank: Gas, 29 gallons; LP gas, 25.1 gallons (80 percent full); diesel, 29 gallons
Cooling System: 4 3/4 gallons
Transmission and Differential: 9 1/2 gallons (includes power steering, hydraulic system, and power brakes)

Clutch: Foot clutch, 11-inch dry disk type, spring loaded
Brakes Hydraulic power brakes, wet disk type, never need adjusting
Electrical System: 12-volt lighting and accessories, 12-volt starter on gasoline and LP gas models, 24-volt starter on diesel
Instrument Panel: Speed-hour meter, electric fuel gauge, oil pressure and generator current indicator, coolant heat indicator, light switch, safety key switch starter. (Tractor must be in neutral to start.)

3010 Series Row-Crop Tractor

Horsepower: 55 horsepower taken at PTO at 2,200 rpm engine speed (factory observed)
Shipping Weight: 5,820 pounds
Engine: Four-cylinder, wet sleeve, valve-in-head
Governed speed range: 600 rpm to 2,200 rpm
Operating speed range: 1,500 rpm to 2,200 rpm
Transport speed range: 2,200 rpm to 2,500 rpm

	Gasoline	LP Gas	Diesel
Bore and stroke (inches):	4x4	4x4	4 1/8x4 3/4
Compression ratios:	7.5 to 1	9.0 to 1	16.4 to 1
Displacement (cubic inches):	201.06	201.06	253.9

Lubrication: Full pressure, full flow with bypass relief valve, replaceable micronic paper element
Cooling: Bypass cooling system with centrifugal pump and thermostatic heat control
Power Take-Off: Independent Dual-Speed Rear PTO (540–1,000 rpm at 1,900 rpm engine

speed); front power take-off for 1,000-rpm equipment

Capacities
Fuel Tank: Gas, 29 gallons; LP gas, 25.1 gallons (80 percent full); diesel, 29 gallons
Cooling System: 4 3/4 gallons
Crankcase: 8 quarts with filter change
Transmission and Differential: 9 1/2 gallons (includes power steering, hydraulic system, and power brakes)

Clutch: Foot clutch, 11-inch dry disk type, spring loaded
Brakes: Hydraulic power brakes, wet disk type, never need adjusting
Electrical System: 12-volt lighting and accessories, 12-volt starter on gasoline and LP gas models, 24-volt starter on diesel
Instrument Panel: Speed-hour meter, electric fuel gauge, oil pressure and generator current indicator, coolant heat indicator, light switch, safety key switch starter (tractor must be in neutral to start)

3010 Series Row-Crop Utility Tractor

Horsepower: 55 horsepower taken at PTO at 2,200 rpm engine speed (factory observed)
Shipping Weight: 5,624 pounds
Engine: Four-cylinder, wet sleeve, valve-in-head
Governed speed range: 600 rpm to 2,200 rpm
Operating speed range: 1,500 rpm to 2,200 rpm
Transport speed range: 2,200 rpm to 2,500 rpm

	Gasoline	LP Gas	Diesel
Bore and stroke (inches):	4x4	4x4	4 1/8x4 3/4
Compression ratios:	7.5 to 1	9.0 to 1	16.4 to 1
Displacement (cubic inches):	201.06	201.06	253.9

Lubrication: Full pressure, full flow with bypass relief valve, replaceable micronic paper element
Cooling: Bypass cooling system with centrifugal pump and thermostatic heat control
Power Take-Off: Independent dual-speed rear PTO (540–1,000 rpm at 1,900-rpm engine speed); front power take-off for 1,000 rpm equipment

Capacities
Fuel Tank: Gasoline, 29 gallons; LP Gas, 25.1 gallons (80 percent full); Diesel, 29 gallons
Cooling System: 4 3/4 gallons
Crankcase: 8 quarts with filter change
Transmission and Differential: 9 1/2 gallons (includes power steering, hydraulic system and power brakes)

Clutch: Foot clutch, 11-inch dry disk type, spring loaded
Brakes: Hydraulic power brakes, wet disk type, never need adjusting
Electrical System: 12-volt lighting and accessories, 12-volt starter on gasoline and LP gas models, 24-volt starter on diesel
Instrument Panel: Speed-hour meter, electric fuel gauge, oil pressure and generator current indicator, coolant heat indicator, light switch, safety key switch starter (Tractor must be in neutral to start.)

3020 Row-Crop Tractor

Horsepower	Gasoline	LP Gas	Diesel
Syncro-Range:	71.37	70.66	71.26
Power Shift:	67.13	64.70	65.23

Maximum observed horsepower measured at the PTO at 2,500 engine rpm in official tests

Shipping Weight: Gas, 7,395 pounds; LP gas, 7,545 pounds; diesel, 7,610 pounds (with equipment for average field service)
Engine: Four-cylinder, variable-speed, wet-sleeve; valve-in-head
Governed speed range: 800 to 2,500 rpm
Operating speed range: 1,500 to 2,500 rpm
Maximum transport speed: 2,500 rpm

	Gasoline	LP Gas	Diesel
Bore and stroke (inches):	4.25x4.25	4.25x4.25	4.25x4.75
Compression ratio:	7.5 to 1	9.0 to 1	16.5 to 1
Displacement (cubic inches):	241	241	269

Lubrication: full-pressure, full-flow filtration with bypass; micronic paper element
Cooling: pressure with centrifugal pump and thermostatic heat control
Air cleaner: dry-type with restriction indicator

Capacities
Fuel tank: Gas, 29 gallons; LP gas, 34 gallons; diesel 29 gallons (80 percent full)
Cooling system: 19 quarts
Crankcase, includes filter: 8 quarts
Transmission, differential, and hydraulic system, at service intervals:
Syncro-Range: 8 gallons

Power Shift: 11 gallons

Power Take-Off: Independent 540–1,000 rpm rear; 1,000 rpm front; hydraulic assist dry-disk on Syncro-Range, hydraulic, multiple wet-disk on Power Shift

Transmission: Syncro-Range: Constant-mesh, helical gears, range-synchronized; eight forward, two reverse;. Power Shift: Multiple wet-disk; hydraulically actuated; eight forward, four reverse

Clutch: Syncro-Range: Foot-operated, spring-loaded, 12-inch dry-disk; Power Shift: Multiple wet-disk, foot-operated (not required for shifting); hand-operated, dry-disk engine disconnect

Hydraulics: closed-center, constant-pressure, variable displacement system

Steering: Full-power, hydrostatic-type; provision for manual operation

Brakes: Full-power, wet-disk type, foot-operated individually or simultaneously; provision for manual operation

Differential Lock: Foot-operated, multiple wet-disk, hydraulically actuated

Electrical System: 12-volt lighting, accessories and starting alternator

Instrument Panel: Speed-hour meter, fuel gauge, engine temperature gauge, engine oil pressure light, alternator light, transmission temperature gauge, transmission oil pressure light (Power Shift), air cleaner restriction light; light switch; key-start switch; cigar lighter; fiber-optic instrument lighting

---

3020 Hi-Crop

Shipping Weight: Gasoline, 7,805 pounds; LP gas, 7,955 pounds; diesel, 8,020 pounds (with equipment for average field service)

Dimensions (with 15.5-38 rear and 7.50-18 front tires)
Wheelbase: 92.8 inches
Overall length: 141.2 inches
Overall width: flange axle, 78 inches; rack axle, 95.5 inches
Height to steering wheel: 92.7 inches
Turning radius (brakes applied): 10 feet
Minimum crop clearance
Front axle: 36.3 inches
Rear axle: 26.9 inches
Rear housing: 36.5 inches
Front wheel treads: 60 to 89.3 inches
Rear wheel treads
Flanged axle: 60 to 98 inches
Rack axle: 73 to 97 inches

4000 Row-Crop Tractor

Horsepower: 94 maximum observed measured at the PTO at 2,200 engine rpm (factory observed)

Shipping Weight: 7,670 pounds

Engine: Six-cylinder gas or diesel, variable-speed, wet-sleeve, valve-in-head
Governed speed range: 800 to 2,200 rpm
Operating speed range: 1,500 to 2,200 rpm
Maximum transport speed: 2,500 rpm

	Gasoline	Diesel
Bore and stroke (inches):	4.25x4.25	4.24x4.75
Compression ratio:	7.5 to 1	16.5 to 1
Displacement (cubic inches):	360	404

Lubrication: Full-pressure, full-flow filtration with bypass; micronic paper element
Cooling: Pressure with centrifugal pump and thermostatic heat control
Air cleaner: Dry-type with restriction indicator and integral precleaner

Capacities
Fuel tank: 34 gallons
Cooling system: 24 quarts
Crankcase (includes filter): Gas, 8 quarts; diesel 12 quarts
Transmission, differential, and hydraulic system (at service intervals): 10 gallons

Power Take-Off: Independent 540 to 1,000 rpm rear at 1,900 engine rpm, with only 540-rpm stub-shaft furnished; hydraulic-assist dry-disk

Transmission: Syncro-range, constant-mesh, helical gears, range-synchronized—eight forward, two reverse

Clutch: Foot-operated, spring-loaded, 12-inch dry-disk

Differential Lock: Foot-operated, multiple wet-disk type, hydraulically actuated

Hydraulics: closed-center, constant-pressure, variable displacement system; rockshaft and single remote cylinder control; additional controls may be field installed

Steering: Full-power, hydrostatic type; provision for manual operation

Brakes: Hydraulic power, wet-disk type, foot-operated individually or simultaneously; provision for manual operation

Throttle: Both hand- and foot-operated

Electrical System: 12-volt lighting, accessories, and starting; alternator

Instrument Panel: Speed-hour meter, fuel gauge, engine-temperature gauge, engine-oil-pressure light, alternator light, air-cleaner light, light switch, neutral key-start switch, cigar lighter

Drawbar: Adjustable swinging

Hitch: Rockshaft and three-point hitch for Category 1 or 2 implements

Fenders and Lights: Single headlights and one combination rear light and flashing warning light on left fender

Front Wheels: Adjustable axle with 9.5L-15, six-ply, F-2 tires

Rear Wheels: Cast wheels with 15.5-38, six-ply, R-1 or 16.9-34, six-ply, R-1 tires

Special Equipment: Remote hydraulic cylinder; Roll-Gard, canopy for Roll-Gard, double front-end weights, rear-wheel weights

---

4010 Series Standard Tractor

Horsepower: 80 horsepower taken at PTO at 2,200 rpm engine speed (factory observed)

Shipping Weight: 6,980 pounds

Engine: Six-cylinder, wet sleeve, valve-in-head
Governed speed range: 600 rpm to 2,200 rpm
Operating speed range: 1,500 rpm to 2,200 rpm
Transport speed range: 2,200 rpm to 2,500 rpm

	Gasoline	LP Gas	Diesel
Bore and stroke (inches):	4x4	4x4	4 1/8x4 3/4
Compression ratios:	7.5 to 1	9.0 to 1	16.4 to l
Displacement (cubic inches):	301.59	301.59	380.8

Lubrication: Full pressure, full flow with bypass relief valve, replaceable micronic paper element
Cooling: Bypass cooling system with centrifugal pump and thermostatic heat control

Power Take-Off: Independent dual-speed rear PTO (540 to 1,000 rpm at 1,900 rpm engine speed); front power take-off for 1,000-rpm equipment

Capacities
Fuel Tank: Gasoline, 34 gallons; LP gas, 39 gallons (80 percent full); diesel, 34 gallons
Cooling System: 6 gallons
Crankcase: 8 quarts with filter change
Transmission and Differential: 11 gallons (includes power steering, hydraulic system, and power brakes)

Clutch: Foot clutch, 12-inch dry disk type, spring loaded

Brakes: Hydraulic power brakes, wet disk type, never need adjusting

Electrical System: 12-volt lighting and accessories, 12-volt starter on gasoline and LP gas models, 24-volt starter on diesel

Instrument Panel: Speed-hour meter, electric fuel gauge, oil pressure and generator current indicator, coolant heat indicator, light switch, safety key switch starter (Tractor must be in neutral to start.)

4010 Series Row-Crop Tractor

Horsepower: 80 horsepower taken at PTO at 2,200 rpm engine speed (factory observed)

Shipping Weight: 6,525 pounds

Engine: Six-cylinder, wet-sleeve, valve-in-head
Governed speed range: 600 to 2,200 rpm
Operating speed range: 1,500 to 2,200 rpm
Transport speed range: 2,200 to 2,500 rpm

	Gasoline	LP Gas	Diesel
Bore and stroke (inches):	4x4	4x4	4 1/8x4 3/4
Compression ratios:	7.5 to 1	9.0 to 1	16.4 to 1
Displacement (cubic inches):	301.59	301.59	380.8

Lubrication: Full pressure, full flow with bypass relief valve, replaceable micronic paper element
Cooling: Bypass cooling system with centrifugal pump and thermostatic heat control

Power Take-Off: Independent Dual-Speed Rear PTO (540–1,000 rpm at 1,900 rpm engine speed); front power take-off for 1,000 rpm equipment

Capacities
Fuel Tank: Gasoline, 34 gallons; LP gas, 39 gallons (80 percent full); diesel, 34 gallons
Cooling System: 6 gallons
Crankcase: 8 quarts with filter change
Transmission and Differential: 11 gallons (includes power steering, hydraulic system, and power brakes)

Clutch: Foot clutch, 12-inch dry disk type, spring loaded

Brakes: Hydraulic power brakes, wet disk type, never need adjusting

Electrical System: 12-volt lighting and accessories, 12-volt starter on gasoline and LP gas models, 24-volt starter on diesel

Instrument Panel: Speed-hour meter, electric fuel gauge, oil pressure and generator current indicator, coolant heat indicator, light switch, safety key switch starter (Tractor must be in neutral to start.)

4010 Series Hi-Crop Tractor

Horsepower: 80 horsepower taken at PTO at 2,200 rpm engine speed (factory observed)

Shipping Weight: 8,250 pounds

Engine: Six-cylinder, wet-sleeve, valve-in-head

Governed speed range: 600 rpm to 2,200 rpm

Operating speed range: 1,500 rpm to 2,200 rpm

Transport speed range: 2,200 rpm to 2,500 rpm

	Gasoline	LP Gas	Diesel
Bore and stroke (inches):	4x4	4x4	4 1/8x4 3/4
Compression ratio:	7.5 to 1	9.0 to 1	16.4 to 1
Displacement (cubic inches):	301.59	301.59	380.8

Lubrication: Full pressure, full flow with bypass relief valve, replaceable micronic paper element

Cooling: Bypass cooling system with centrifugal pump and thermostatic heat control

Power Take-Off: Independent Dual-Speed Rear PTO (540–1,000 rpm at 1,900 rpm engine speed); front power take-off for 1,000 rpm equipment

Capacities

Fuel Tank: Gasoline, 34 gallons; LP gas 39 gallons (80 percent full); diesel, 34 gallons

Cooling System: 6 gallons

Crankcase: 8 quarts with filter change

Transmission and Differential: 11 quarts

Final Drive Housing (includes power steering, hydraulic system, and power brakes): 7 quarts (3 1/2 each)

Clutch: Foot clutch, 12-inch dry-disk type, spring loaded

Brakes: Hydraulic power brakes, wet disk type, never need adjusting

Electrical System: 12-volt lighting and accessories, 12-volt starter on gasoline and LP gas models, 24-volt starter on diesel

Instrument Panel: Speed-hour meter, electric fuel gauge, oil pressure and generator current indicator, coolant heat indicator, light switch, safety key switch starter (Tractor must be in neutral to start.)

4020 Row-Crop Tractor

Horsepower

	Gasoline	LP Gas	Diesel
Syncro-Range:	96.66	94.57	94.88
Power Shift:	95.66	90.48	91.17

Maximum observed horsepower measured at the PTO at 2,200 engine rpm in official tests

Shipping Weight: Gas, 8,305 pounds; LP gas, 8,490 pounds; diesel, 8,555 pounds (with equipment for average field service)

Engine: Six-cylinder, variable-speed, wet-sleeve, valve-in-head

Governed speed range: 800 rpm to 2,200 rpm

Operating speed range: 1,500 rpm to 2,200 rpm

Maximum transport speed: 2,500 rpm

	Gasoline	LP Gas	Diesel
Bore and stroke (inches):	4.25x4.25	4.25x4.25	4.25x4.75
Compression ratio:	7.5 to 1	9.0 to 1	16.5 to 1
Displacement (cubic inches):	360	360	404

Lubrication: Full-pressure, full-flow filtration with bypass; micronic paper element

Cooling: Pressure with centrifugal pump and thermostatic heat control

Air cleaner: Dry-type with restriction indicator

Capacities

Fuel tank: Gas, 34 gallons; LP gas, 45 gallons; diesel 34 gallons (80 percent full)

Cooling system: 24 quarts

Crankcase, includes filter: Gas and LP gas, 8 quarts; diesel, 12 quarts

Transmission, differential, and hydraulic system (at service intervals): Syncro-Range, 10 gallons; Power Shift, 14 gallons

Power Take-Off: Independent 540–1,000 rpm rear; 1,000 rpm front; hydraulic assist dry-disk on Syncro-Range; Hydraulic, multiple wet-disk on Power Shift

Transmission: Syncro-Range: Constant-mesh, helical gears, range-synchronized; eight forward, two reverse; Power Shift: Multiple wet-disk; hydraulically actuated; eight forward, four reverse

Clutch: Syncro-Range: Foot-operated, spring-loaded, 12-inch dry-disk; Power Shift: multiple wet-disk, foot-operated (not required for shifting); hand-operated, dry-disk engine disconnect

Hydraulics: Closed-center, constant-pressure, variable displacement system

Steering: Full-power, hydrostatic-type; provision for manual operation

Brakes: Full-power, wet-disk type, foot-operated individually or simultaneously; provision for manual operation

Differential Lock: Foot-operated, multiple wet-disk, hydraulically actuated

Electrical System: 12-volt lighting, accessories, and starting; alternator

Instrument Panel: Speed-hour meter, fuel gauge, engine temperature gauge, engine oil pressure light, alternator light, transmission temperature gauge, transmission oil pres-sure light (Power Shift), air cleaner light; light-switch; key start switch; cigar lighter; fiber-optic instrument lighting

---

4020 Hi-Crop

Horsepower

	Gasoline	LP Gas	Diesel
Syncro-Range:	96.66	94.57	94.88
Power Shift:	95.66	90.48	91.17

Maximum observed horsepower measured at the PTO at 2,200 engine rpm

Shipping Weight: Gasoline, 8,985 pounds; LP gas, 9,170 pounds; diesel 9,235 pounds (with equipment for average field service)

Engine: Six-cylinder, variable-speed, wet-sleeve, valve-in-head

Governed speed range: 800 rpm to 2,200 rpm

Operating speed range: 1,500 rpm to 2,200 rpm

Maximum transport speed: 2,500 rpm

	Gasoline	LP Gas	Diesel
Bore and stroke (inches):	4.25x4.25	4.25x4.25	4.25x4.75
Compression ratio:	7.5 to 1	9.0 to 1	16.5 to 1
Displacement (cubic inches):	360	360	404

Lubrication: Full-pressure, full-flow filtration with bypass; micronic paper element

Cooling: Pressure with centrifugal pump and thermostatic heat control

Air cleaner: Dry-type with restriction indicator

Capacities

Fuel tank: Gas, 34 gallons; LP gas, 45 gallons; diesel, 34 gallons (80 percent full)

Cooling system: 24 quarts

Crankcase, includes filter: Gas and LP gas, 8 quarts; diesel, 12 quarts

Transmission, differential, and hydraulic system, at service intervals: Syncro-Range, 10 gallons; Power Shift, 14 gallons

Power Take-Off: Independent 540 to 1,000 rpm rear; 1,000-rpm front; hydraulic assist dry-disk on Syncro-Range; Hydraulic multiple wet-disk on Power Shift

Transmission: Syncro-Range: Constant-mesh, helical gears, range-synchronized; eight forward, two reverse; Power Shift: Multiple wet-disk; hydraulically actuated; eight forward, four reverse

Clutch: Syncro-Range: Foot-operated, spring-loaded, 12-inch dry-disk; Power Shift: Multiple wet-disk, foot-operated (not required for shifting); hand-operated, dry-disk engine disconnect

Hydraulics: Closed-center, constant-pressure, variable displacement system

Steering: Full-power, hydrostatic-type; provision for manual operation

Brakes: Full-power, wet-disk type, foot-operated individually or simultaneously; provision for manual operation

Differential Lock: Foot-operated, multiple wet-disk, hydraulically actuated

Electrical System: 12-volt lighting, accessories and starting; alternator

Instrument Panel: Speed-hour meter, fuel gauge, engine temperature gauge, engine oil pressure light, alternator light, transmission temperature gauge, transmission oil pres-sure light (Power Shift), air cleaner light; light-switch; key start switch; cigar lighter; fiber-optic instrument lighting

---

4320 and 4620

Horsepower:

	4320 Diesel	4620 Diesel
Syncro-Range:	115	135
Power Shift:	NA	135

(Maximum observed horsepower measured at the PTO at 2,200 engine rpm, factory-observed)

Shipping Weight: 4320 Diesel, 9,050 pounds; 4620 Diesel, 12,980 pounds (with equipment for average field service)

Engine Six-cylinder, variable-speed, wet-sleeve, valve-in-head, turbocharged (4620 has manifold intercooler.)

Governed speed range: 800 to 2,200 rpm

Operating speed range: 1,500 to 2,200 rpm

Maximum transport speed: 2,500 rpm

Bore and stroke: 4.25x4.75 inches

Compression ratio: 4320 Diesel, 15.7 to 1; 4620 Diesel, 16.4 to 1

Displacement (cubic inches): 404

Lubrication: Full-pressure, full-flow with bypass, Micronic paper element

Cooling: Pressure with centrifugal pump and thermostatic heat control

Air cleaner: Dry-type with safety element

Capacities

	4320 Diesel	4620 Diesel
Fuel tank:	44 gallons	50 gallons
Cooling system:	28 quarts	28 quarts
Crankcase, includes filter:	6 quarts	16 quarts

Transmission, differential and hydraulic system (at service intervals): 4320 Diesel: 14 gallons; 4620 Diesel: 18 gallons (Syncro-Range), 16 gallons (Power Shift)

Clutch: Syncro-Range: Foot-operated, spring-loaded, 13.5-inches dry-disk, 14.75-inches dry-disk. Power Shift: multiple wet-disk foot-operated (not required for shifting); hand-operated, dry-disk engine disconnect

Transmission: Syncro-Range: constant-mesh, helical gears, range-synchronized forward gears, eight forward, two reverse. Power-Shift: multiple wet-disk, hydraulically actuated; eight forward, four reverse

Power Take-Off: 4320: Independent 540–1,000 rpm rear at 1,900 engine rpm; hydraulic assist dry-disk. 4620: Independent 1,000- rpm rear at 1,900 engine rpm; hydraulic assist dry-disk on Syncro-Range; hydraulic, multiple wet-disk on Power Shift

Hydraulics: Closed-center, constant-pressure, variable-displacement system

Steering: Full-power, hydrostatic-type; provision for manual operation

Brakes: Full-power, wet-disk type, foot-operated individually or simultaneously; provision for manual operation

Differential Lock: Foot-operated, multiple wet-disk hydraulically actuated

Electrical System: 12-volt lighting, accessories, and starting, with alternator

Instrument Panel: Speed-hour meter, fuel gauge, engine-temperature gauge, engine-oil-pressure light, alternator indicator light, transmission-temperature gauge, transmission-oil-pressure light (Power Shift), air cleaner indicator light, light switch, safety key start switch, cigar lighter, fiber-optic instrument lighting, high-beam indicator light

Standard Equipment: Turbo-Built, six-cylinder, variable-speed, diesel engine; Syncro-Range Transmission, eight forward and two reverse gears; 22 gallons per minute pump for all hydraulic functions; Power Steering; Power Brakes; single remote-cylinder control; rockshaft with three-point hitch (Quik-Coupler Hitch on 4620); adjustable drawbar; power-engaged 540–1,000 rpm rear PTO on 4320, 1,000 rpm on 4620; row-crop fenders with dual-beam lights and foot-operated dimmer switch; rear combination field-and-road light; two flashing warning lights; Deluxe Seat; adjustable front axle; hand and foot-throttle; alternator; speed-hour meter; electric fuel gauge; dry air-cleaner with integral precleaner and safety element; full-flow oil filter; upright muffler with cover; anti-freeze; front tires: 10.00-16, six-ply, F-2; rear tires: 18.4-38, six-ply, R-1 on heavy cast wheels, 4320; 18.4-38, ten-ply, R-1 on heavy cast wheels, 4620; regular rack-and-pinion rear axle

4520

Horsepower: Syncro-Range, 123.39; Power Shift, 122.36; maximum observed horsepower measured at the PTO at 2,200 engine rpm in official tests

Shipping Weight: 12,285 pounds (with equipment for average field service)

Engine: Six-cylinder diesel, variable-speed, wet-sleeve, valve-in-head, turbocharged
Governed speed range: 800 to 2,200 rpm
Operating speed range: 1,500 to 2,200 rpm
Maximum transport speed: 2,500 rpm
Bore and stroke: 4.25x4.75 inches
Compression ratio: 16.4 to 1
Displacement: 404 cubic inches
Lubrication: Full-pressure, full-flow filtration with bypass; micronic paper element
Cooling: Pressure with centrifugal pump and thermostatic heat control
Air cleaner: Dry-type with restriction indicator

Capacities
Fuel tank: 50 gallons
Cooling system: 28 quarts
Crankcase, includes filter: 14 quarts
Transmission, differential, and hydraulic system (At service intervals)
Syncro-Range: 18 gallons
Power Shift: 16 gallons

Power Take-Off: Independent 1,000-rpm, rear; 1,000-rpm, front; hydraulic assist dry disk on Syncro-Range; hydraulic, multiple wet-disk on Power Shift

Transmission: Syncro-Range: constant-mesh, helical-gears, range-synchronized; eight forward, two reverse Power Shift: Multiple wet-disk; hydraulically actuated; eight forward, four reverse

Clutch: Syncro-Range: foot-operated, spring-loaded, 14.75-inch dry-disk. Power Shift: Multiple wet-disk, foot-operated (not required for shifting); hand-operated, dry-disk engine disconnect

Hydraulics: Closed-center, constant-pressure, variable-displacement system

Steering: Full-power, hydrostatic-type; provision for manual operation

Brakes: Full-power, wet-disk type, foot-operated individually or simultaneously; provision for manual operation

Differential Lock: Foot-operated, multiple wet-disk, hydraulically actuated

Electrical System: 12-volt lighting, accessories, and starting; alternator

Instrument Panel: Speed-hour meter, fuel gauge, engine-temperature gauge, engine oil-pressure light, alternator light, transmission-temperature gauge; transmission oil-pressure light (Power Shift), air-cleaner restriction light; light-switch; key start switch; cigar lighter; fiber-optic instrument lighting

4520 Row-Crop

Horsepower: Syncro-Range, 123.39; Power Shift, 122.36. Maximum observed horsepower measured at the PTO at 2,200 engine rpm in official tests

Shipping Weight: 12,285 pounds (with equipment for average field service)

Engine: Six-cylinder diesel, variable-speed, wet-sleeve, valve-in-head, turbocharged
Governed speed range: 800 to 2,200 rpm
Operating speed range: 1,500 to 2,200 rpm
Maximum transport speed: 2,500 rpm
Bore and stroke: 4.25x4.75 inches
Compression ratio: 16.4 to 1
Displacement: 404 cubic inches
Lubrication: Full-pressure, full-flow filtration with bypass; micronic paper element
Cooling: Pressure with centrifugal pump and thermostatic heat control
Air cleaner: Dry-type with restriction indicator

Capacities
Fuel tank: 50 gallons
Cooling system: 28 quarts
Crankcase, includes filter: 14 quarts
Transmission, differential, and hydraulic system (At service intervals)
Syncro-Range: 18 gallons
Power Shift: 16 gallons

Power Take-Off: Independent 1,000-rpm rear; 1,000-rpm front; hydraulic assist dry-disk on Syncro-Range; hydraulic, multiple wet-disk on Power Shift

Transmission: Syncro-Range: constant-mesh, helical-gears, range-synchronized; eight forward, two reverse Power Shift: Multiple wet-disk; hydraulically actuated; eight forward, four reverse

Clutch: Syncro-Range: foot-operated, spring-loaded, 14.75-inch dry-disk. Power Shift: Multiple wet-disk, foot-operated (not required for shifting). Hand-operated, dry-disk engine disconnect

Hydraulics: Closed-center, constant-pressure, variable-displacement system

Steering: Full-power, hydrostatic-type; provision for manual operation

Brakes: Full-power, wet-disk type, foot-operated individually or simultaneously; provision for manual operation

Differential Lock: Foot-operated, multiple wet-disk, hydraulically actuated

Electrical System: 12-volt lighting, accessories, and starting

Instrument Panel: Speed-hour meter, fuel gauge, engine-temperature gauge, engine oil-pressure light, alternator light, transmission-temperature gauge; transmission oil-pressure light (Power Shift), air-cleaner restriction light; light-switch; key start switch; cigar lighter; fiber-optic instrument lighting

5010

Horsepower: 117 horsepower taken at PTO at 2,200 rpm engine speed (factory observed). Not tested at Nebraska

Shipping Weight: 16,600 pounds (with equipment for average field service)

Engine: Six-cylinder, wet-sleeve, valve-in-head
Governed speed range: 600 rpm to 2,500 rpm
Operating speed range: 1,500 rpm to 2,200 rpm
Transport speed range: 2,200 rpm to 2,500 rpm
Bore and stroke: 4 3/4x5 inches
Displacement: 531 cubic inches
Lubrication: Full pressure, full flow with bypass relief valve, replaceable micronic paper element
Cooling: Bypass cooling system with centrifugal pump and thermostatic heat control
Compression ratio: 16.1 to 1

Capacities
Fuel tank: 48 gallons
Cooling system: 37 quarts
Crankcase: 12 quarts
Transmission and hydraulic system: 16 gallons

Power Take-Off: Independent rear PTO for 1,000 rpm operation at 1,900 engine rpm

Clutch: Foot clutch, two heavy-duty 11-inch dry disk plates

Brakes: Hydraulic power brakes, wet disk-type

Electric System: 24-volt system with four 6-volt dry-charge batteries, 12-volt lighting and accessories

Instrument Panel: Speed-hour meter, electric fuel gauge; oil pressure, generator current, and coolant heat indicators; light switch; safety key starter (Tractor must be in neutral to start.)

5020

Horsepower: 140 maximum observed horsepower measured at PTO at 2,200 engine rpm (factory observed)

Shipping Weight: 15,600 pounds (with equipment for average field service)
Engine: Six-cylinder, wet-sleeve, valve-in-head, variable speed, diesel
    Speed ranges: Governed range, 800 to 2,500 rpm; operating range, 1,500 to 2,200 rpm; maximum transport speed, 2,500 rpm
    Bore and stroke: 4.75x5 inches
    Displacement: 531 cubic inches
    Compression ratio: 16.5 to 1
    Lubrication: Full-pressure, full-flow with bypass relief valve; replaceable micronic paper element
    Cooling: Bypass cooling system with centrifugal pump and thermostatic heat control
Capacities
    Fuel tank: 68 gallons
    Cooling system: 33 quarts
    Crankcase, includes filter: 21 quarts
    Transmission, differential, and hydraulic system (at service interval): 16 gallons
Power Take-Off: Independent rear PTO for 1,000 rpm operation at 1,900 engine rpm
Clutch: Foot-operated, two 12-inch heavy-duty dry-disk type plates, spring-loaded
Brakes: Hydraulic power brakes, wet-disk type
Electrical System: 12-volt starting, lighting and accessories; alternator and transistorized regulator
Instrument Panel: Speed-hour meter; electric fuel gauge; air cleaner, oil-pressure and alternator indicators; coolant-temperature gauge; light switch; key-start switch; cigar lighter

5020 Row-Crop

Horsepower: 140 maximum observed horsepower measured at PTO at 2,200 engine rpm (factory observed)
Shipping Weight: 14,480 pounds (with equipment for average field service)
Engine: Six-cylinder, wet-sleeve, valve-in-head, variable speed, diesel
    Speed ranges: Governed range, 800 to 2,500 rpm; operating range, 1,500 to 2,200 rpm; Maximum transport speed, 2,500 rpm
    Bore and stroke: 4.75x5 inches
    Displacement: 531 cubic inches
    Compression ratio: 16.5 to 1
    Lubrication: Full-pressure, full-flow with bypass relief valve; replaceable micronic paper element
    Cooling: Bypass cooling system with centrifugal pump and thermostatic heat control
Capacities
    Fuel tank: 68 gallons
    Cooling system: 33 quarts
    Crankcase, includes filter: 20 quarts
    Transmission, differential, and hydraulic system (at service interval): 16 gallons
Power Take-Off: Independent rear PTO for 1,000 rpm operation at 1,900 engine rpm
Clutch: Foot-operated, two 12-inch heavy-duty, dry-disk type plates, spring-loaded
Brakes: Hydraulic power brakes, wet-disk type
Electrical System: 12-volt starting, lighting and accessories; alternator and transistorized regulator
Instrument Panel: Speed-hour meter; electric fuel gauge; air cleaner, oil-pressure and alternator indicators; coolant-temperature gauge; light switch; key-start switch; cigar lighter

6030

Horsepower: 175 PTO maximum observed measured at 2,100 rpm
Shipping Weight: Row Crop, 14,680 pounds; standard, 15,800 pounds
Engine: Six-cylinder, variable-speed, wet-sleeve, valve-in-head, turbocharged, intercooled
    Governed speed range: 800 to 2,100 rpm
    Operating speed range: 1,500 to 2,100 rpm
    Maximum transport speed: 2,500 rpm
    Bore and stroke: 4.75x5.0 inches
    Compression ratio: 15.5 to 1
    Displacement cubic inches: 531 cubic inches
    Lubrication: Full pressure, full flow filtration
    Cooling: Pressure with centrifugal pump
    Air cleaner: Dry-type with safety element
Capacities
    Fuel tank: 73 gallons
    Cooling system: 40 quarts
    Crankcase, includes filter: 26 quarts
    Transmission, differential, and hydraulic system: 16 gallons
Power Take-Off: Independent 1,000 rpm (1 3/4 inches diameter shaft)
Transmission: Constant-mesh, eight forward, two reverse

Clutch: Spring-loaded, two 13 1/2-inch dry-disk
Hydraulics: Closed-center, constant-pressure, variable-displacement
Steering: Full power, hydrostatic
Brakes: Full power, wet-disk
Differential Lock: Foot-operated, multiple wet disk, hydraulically actuated
Electrical System: 12-volt with alternator

7020

Horsepower: 146 maximum horsepower observed at the PTO at 2,200 engine rpm (factory observed)
Shipping Weight: 14,580 pounds (with equipment for average field service)
Engine: Six-cylinder, variable-speed, wet-sleeve, valve-in-head, turbocharged diesel with intercooler
    Governed speed range: 800 to 2,200 rpm
    Operating speed range: 1,500 to 2,200 rpm
    Maximum transport speed: 2,500 engine rpm
    Bore and stroke: 4.25x4.75 inches
    Compression ratio: 16.4 to 1
    Displacement: 404 cubic inches
    Lubrication: Full-pressure, full-flow filtration with bypass; micronic paper element
    Cooling: Pressure with centrifugal pump and thermostatic heat control
    Air cleaner: Dry-type with safety element
Capacities
    Fuel tank: 156 gallons
    Cooling system: 32 quarts
    Crankcase, includes filter: 20 quarts
    Transmission, rear differential and hydraulic system: 19 gallons
    Front differential: 5 gallons
Power Take-Off: Transmission-driven 1,000-rpm, rear
Transmission: Syncro-Range: constant-mesh type with helical-gears, range-synchronized and optional high-low; 16 forward, 4 reverse speeds
Clutch: Foot-operated, spring-loaded, two 14.75-inch dry-disk
Hydraulics: Closed-center, constant-pressure, variable-displacement system with two selective control valves
Steering: Full-power, articulated steering, hydrostatic type with dual, single-action, hydraulic cylinders; provision for manual operation
Brakes: Full-power, wet-disk type, rear brakes, foot-operated; provision for manual operation
Electrical System: 12-volt lighting, accessories, and starting with alternator
Instrument Panel: Speed-hour meter, fuel gauge, engine-temperature gauge, engine-oil-pressure light, alternator light, transmission-temperature gauge, air cleaner-restriction light, light switch, key-start switch, cigar lighter, fiber-optic instrument lighting, fluid-starting aid adapter

7520

Horsepower: 175 maximum horsepower observed at the PTO at 2,100 engine rpm (factory observed)
Shipping Weight: 16,790 pounds (with equipment for average field service)
Engine: Six-cylinder, variable-speed, wet-sleeve, valve-in-head, turbocharged diesel with intercooler
    Governed speed range: 800 to 2,100 rpm
    Operating speed range: 1,500 to 2,100 rpm
    Maximum transport speed: 2,500 engine rpm
    Bore and stroke: 4.75x5.00 inches
    Compression ratio: 15.5 to 1
    Displacement: 531 cubic inches
    Lubrication: Full-pressure, full-flow filtration with bypass; micronic paper element
    Cooling: Pressure with centrifugal pump and thermostatic heat control
    Air cleaner: Dry-type with safety element
Capacities
    Fuel tank: 156 gallons
    Cooling system: 40 quarts
    Crankcase, includes filter: 26 quarts
    Transmission, rear differential and hydraulic system: 19 gallons
    Front differential: 5 gallons
Power Take-Off: Transmission-driven 1,000-rpm, rear
Transmission: Syncro-Range: constant-mesh type with helical-gears, range-synchronized and optional high-low; 16 forward, 4 reverse speeds
Clutch: Foot-operated, spring-loaded, two 14.75-inch dry-disk
Hydraulics: Closed-center, constant-pressure, variable-displacement system with two selective control valves

Steering: Full-power, articulated steering, hydrostatic type with dual, single-action, hydraulic cylinders; provision for manual operation

Brakes: Full-power, wet-disk type, rear brakes, foot-operated; provision for manual operation

Electrical system: 12-volt lighting, accessories, and starting with alternator

Instrument panel: Speed-hour meter, fuel gauge, engine-temperature gauge, engine-oil-pressure light, alternator light, transmission-temperature gauge, air cleaner-restriction light, light switch, key-start switch, cigar lighter, fiber-optic instrument lighting, fluid-starting aid adapter

---

8010

Horsepower: Not tested at Nebraska (Engine—206 horsepower (corrected) with air cleaner and muffler)

Engine: GM C671E, two-cycle, six-cylinder diesel
Bore and stroke: 4.25x5.00 inches
Compression ratio: 17 to 1
Displacement: 425 cubic inches
RPM (rated full load): 2,100
Fuel system: Recirculating bleed type with full-flow fuel filter
Lubricating: Full pressure force feed system with full-flow oil filter and bypass filter
Cooling: Bypass-type pressure cooling system

Clutch: Heavy-duty, four-plate hydraulically actuated

Brakes: Four-wheel air brakes

Capacities
Fuel tank: 106 gallons
Hydraulic reservoir: 25 gallons
Cooling system: 12 gallons
Crankcase: 4 1/2 gallons
Transmission: 2 gallons
Drop housing case: 1 gallon
Axle housing and planetary: 7 gallons

Hydraulic System: Two- or three-function with 40- or 60-gallon-per-minute pump. Three-point hitch available

Electrical System: 24-volt starting system; 12 volts for lights and accessories, four front lights, two head and two flood; four rear lights, two red tail and two flood

Wheel Equipment: Two 36,500 series clark axles

Other Standard Equipment: Engine tachometer, hour meter, speedometer, cigarette lighter, heavy-duty swinging drawbar, extra-wide foam cushion seat, ether starting aid, power steering with 5x16 inches double-acting cylinder with 40 gallon-per-minute pump

---

8020

Horsepower: 200-plus engine horsepower, 150 drawbar horsepower. Not tested at Nebraska

Engine: GM 671E, two-cycle, six-cylinder diesel
Bore and stroke: 4.25x5.00 inches
Compression ratio: 17 to 1
Displacement: 425 cubic inches
RPM (rated full load): 2100
Fuel system: Recirculating bleed type with full-flow fuel filter
Lubricating: Full pressure force feed system with full-flow oil filter and bypass filter
Cooling: Bypass-type pressure cooling system

Capacities
Fuel tank: 106 gallons
Transmission and clutch housing: 15 gallons
Hydraulic reservoir: 25 gallons
Axle housing and planetary: 9 gallons
Cooling system: 12 gallons
Air cleaner: 1 4/5 gallons
Crankcase: 4 1/2 gallons
Steering gear housing: 1/5 gallon

Clutch: Oil cooled, heavy-duty, four-plate hydraulically actuated

Brakes: Four-wheel air brakes, mechanical parking brake

Hydraulic System: Two or three-function with 40- or 60-gallon-per-minute pump. Three-point hitch available

Electrical System: 24-volt starting system; 12 volts for lights and accessories. Four front lights, two head and two flood; four rear lights, two red tail and two flood

Wheel Equipment: (Two 36,500 series clark axles) 23.1-26 12-ply on 20-inch rims

Other Standard Equipment: Posture-design seat, engine tachometer, speedometer, cigarette lighter, ether starting aid, power steering with 5x6-inch double-acting cylinder, heavy-duty swinging drawbar

---

8020 Diesel Tractor

Horsepower: 31 maximum observed horsepower at the PTO at 2,100 engine rpm (factory estimate)

Shipping Weight: 4,350 pounds (with equipment for average field service)

Engine: Three-cylinder vertical, valve-in-head, four-stroke diesel
Speed ranges: Governed range: 650 to 2,400 rpm; operating range: 1,400 to 2,100 rpm; transport range: 2,100 to 2,400 rpm
Bore and stroke: 3.86x4.3 inches
Compression ratio: 16.7 to 1
Displacement: 151.9 cubic inches
Lubrication: Pressure system with full-flow oil filter
Cooling: Pressurized with pump, thermostat, and fixed bypass

Capacities
Fuel tank: 16.5 gallons
Cooling system: 2.75 gallons
Crankcase: 1.50 gallons
Transmission, differential, and hydraulic system: 10 gallons

Power Take-Off: Continuous-running (live) 540-rpm rear PTO

Clutch: Dual-stage clutch with 10-inch transmission disk and 9-inch PTO disk

Brakes: Hydraulically actuated, foot-operated individually or simultaneously

Electrical System: 12-volt starting and lighting equipment

ASAE PTO Speed: 2,100 rpm

Base Equipment: Three-cylinder diesel engine collar shift transmission with eight forward, four reverse selections; 12-volt starter and electric system; key ignition and push-button starter; fenders; manual steering; rear-exhaust muffler; oil-bath air cleaner; formed-steel seat with pad; speed hour meter; two front lights and fender-mounted warning lamp; adjustable swept-back front axle oil-pressure indicator light; coolant-temperature gauge; generator indicator light; eight-position steel rear wheels; hand- and foot-throttle controls; starting fluid adapter; antifreeze; differential lock swinging drawbar; rockshaft and Category 1, three-point hitch; 540-rpm continuous-running power take-off; hydraulic pump for open-center hydraulic system; 12.4-28, four-ply rear and 6.00-16, four-ply front tires

Special Equipment: Deluxe seat; single-action remote cylinder circuit with rear outlet for one cylinder; upright exhaust muffler; front-end and rear-wheel weights 11.2-28, four-ply, or 12.428, six-ply; 13.6-28, four-ply rear tires 5.50-16, four-ply, or 6.0016, six-ply front tires; power steering

BIBLIOGRAPHY

American Society of Agricultural Engineers. *John Deere Tractors, 1918–1994*. St. Joseph, Michigan: American Society of Agricultural Engineers, 1994.

Broehl, Wayne G. Jr. *John Deere's Company*. New York: Doubleday and Company, 1984.

Huber, Donald S. and Ralph C. Hughes. *How Johnny Popper Replaced the Horse*. Moline, Illinois. Deere & Company, 1988.

Leffingwell, Randy. *John Deere Farm Tractors*. Osceola, Wisconsin: Motorbooks International, 1993.

Macmillan, Don and Russell Jones. *John Deere Tractors and Equipment, Vol. 1*. St. Joseph, Michigan: American Society of Agricultural Engineers, 1988.

Macmillan, Don and Roy Harrington. *John Deere Tractors and Equipment, Vol. 2*. St. Joseph, Michigan: American Society of Agricultural Engineers, 1991.

Macmillan, Don. *John Deere Tractors Worldwide*. St. Joseph, Michigan: American Society of Agricultural Engineers, 1994.

Mills, Robert K. *Implement and Tractor: Reflection on 100 Years of Farm Equipment*. Overland Park, Kansas: Intertec Publishing, 1986.

———*John Deere Company: Kansas City Branch*. Moline, Illinois: Deere & Company, 1994.

———*Tractor Digest*. Vol. 1, No. 2. Eldora, Iowa: Tytonidae Publishing Company, 1994.

———*Tractor Digest*. Vol. 2, No. 1. Eldora, Iowa: Tytonidae Publishing Company, 1995.

INDEX